On the *Other* Hand

By Steve Anderson, PGA

with Paul deVere

Photography by Lori Salem
Cover photo by John Burns

Saron Press, Ltd.
Hilton Head Island, South Carolina

Dedication

To my wife, Karen and baby boy Parker Griffen Anderson ("PGA"). It is for you that I do everything in my life. I love you both more than words can say.

To my mother and father, Joan and Don Anderson. You are the greatest parents anyone could ever ask for and have always been a shining example in my life.

To my sister, Susan. As mom and dad have always said, both of us are lucky to be doing exactly what we dreamed of in life. I'm very proud of your accomplishments with the symphony.

To mom and dad Grimes. I'm thankful everyday to be part of your extended family.

To my dearest friend, Greg (Leg) Lacy. "Just a pair of knickers, then please."

To Lefty Barba, for getting me started in this game. You are truly an example of what a PGA professional should be and your knowledge, wisdom and friendship have stayed with me for more than 20 years.

To Ken Venturi. Thanks for the knowledge and tremendous opportunity you gave me, and what you mean to the game of golf.

ISBN 0-9650791-4-7
Library of Congress Control Number: 2001119552

First Printing, December 2001
Second Printing, August 2002

Designed by Michael Reinsch Design, Hilton Head Island, SC.

Printed by RJ Communications, L.L.C., New York, NY

What They're Saying About
On the Other Hand & Steve Anderson!

"Steve Anderson's *On the Other Hand* is the equivalent of Harvey Penicks Little Red Book for lefty golfers. No left-handed golfer should be without it."
-- *L.A.Wodrich, WALG*

"Anderson's book is an essential for lefty golfers at all levels of play. It covers everything lefties need to know to improve their game and consistently shoot lower scores. Simply excellent instruction."
-- *Mark Johnson, Founder, Left-Tee Golf.com*

"Steve Anderson definitely deserves a pat on the back. Good, solid instruction. *On the Other Hand* is a 'must read' for left-handed hitters."
-- *John Richardson, Head Professional, Sea Pines Resort, Hilton Head Island, SC*

"I am a 71 year young male lefty who recently started playing again after many years of inactivity. (After reading the book) the improvement in my game is so dramatic I can't put it into words. My advice to lefties, buy this book. .
-- *D. C. Morris*

"Steve, your book really helped me with my game. I have been practicing for several months and just played my first 18 holes - I pared 3 of the first 7 holes and just missed a hole in one!
-- *Tom Peters Scottsdale, AZ*

"Steve's book is a diamond in the rough --no pun intended -- for the left-handed golfers who have tried in vain to understand the golf swing from the right-handed perspective. This book will give every left-handed golfer an equal opportunity to compete on the same course as their right-handed rivals."
-- *Leigh Taylor, Director of Golf, Springfield Healthplex PGA Master Professional PGA Life Member*

"*On The Other Hand* is a fantastic instructional manual that has helped improve my game better than my more expensive clubs!. I am not an expert, but I think this golf book is going to be 'HOT!' "
-- *Gus Caniff Washington, DC*

"Hurray for Steve Anderson's new book, "*On the Other Hand*." I'm a right-handed player, but had seen some of Steve's tips in various golf magazines over the years, and was anxious to read his first

book. I was not disappointed! The chapter on the full swing was great, and I loved the common sense explanations he gave."
-- *Kevin A. Kyle,*
Fort Myers, FL

"Having read many golf books I feel qualified to comment. Steve's book breaks the full swing and short game down into manageable and understandable pieces. The pictures in the book make the instruction more understandable. My scores have definitely improved by implementing the instruction techniques contained in *On the Other Hand.*"
-- *L. Schoenfeld*
Fort Myers, FL

"All I can say is 'Thank you' Steve Anderson.After years of having to flip all the images and reverse all the words, Steves book presents a wonderfully, clear picture of the golf swing."
-- *Tom Prentiss*
Myrtle Beach, SC

"Steve Anderson's new book *On the Other Hand* is a must read for all left handed golfers. Steve breaks down the full swing into three key fundamentals that are easy to understand. His discussion of the short game is concise and simple to follow."
--*B. McConnell*
Fort Myers, FL

"At last a book I can call my own. Steve's book of golf instruction is wonderful. The chapter on the 3 fundamentals make so much sense that my golf (for the first time) seems almost to simple. I give it 10 stars!"
-- *Brian Garavuso,*
Washington, DC

"I give *On the Other Hand* 5 stars. I've never read a golf book that outlined so clearly what I'am supposed to do with my golf swing. Nice job!"
--*George Landon,*
Fort Myers, FL

"After years of taking lessons and working on my game (with not much success), I met Steve when he worked for Ken Venturi. His instruction helped me so dramatically I came to visit him the next year, and the next after that. No small task considering it's an 1800-mile trek. What I learned from him on the lesson tee was worth every penny, and I consider Steve one of the game's premier teachers."
-- *Wayne Morris,*
Newfoundland, Canada.

"Three cheers for *On the Other Hand!* I've never played the game better."
-- *Drew Towne*
Falmouth, Cornwall, England

On the *Other* Hand
Table of Contents

Introduction

Because *On the Other Hand* is written by a Certified left-handed PGA teaching professional for left-handed golfers, it could be considered "the first of its kind." But what is more important to me is that lefthanders finally have a book to call their own. No more translations like, "left is really right and right is really..."

Not too long ago, one of my left-handed students brought me a golf instruction book that was very dog-eared and considerably marked up. Page by page, he had gone through the book replacing every "right" with "left" and every "left" with "right" with a felt-tipped pen. I'm not sure, but that could have been the final impetus for *On the Other Hand*.

While I do not think of lefthanders as "victims," it did take golf manufacturers almost a century to figure out there might be a real market for left-handed clubs. (Thank you, Phil Mickelson, even though you're a right-hander in everything else you do.) When I mentioned to one of my left-handed students that I was writing this book, he suggested the title, "It's About Time!" We chuckled. We have both survived in a right-handed world quite well.

The easiest way to use *On the Other Hand* is to think that you are one of my students, standing with me on the practice tee. Consider each chapter a personal lesson. If you take the time to hold your club and follow along each step of the way, I know you will easily understand what I am going to show you.

The instruction presented in this book is filled with easy, logical explanations of what you need to do to hit the ball properly. I have included many analogies to help you understand what I'm showing you. Common sense always prevails in these techniques, and my highest priority is to give you a clear explanation of the movements in the swing.

Are there advantages or disadvantages to being left-handed? My answer: Yes and no. As little as ten years ago, the major club manufactures didn't offer much in the way of quality left-handed clubs. If they had any lefty clubs at all, they usually weren't top of the line. There simply wasn't the broad range of choices that were available to the right-handed player.

But all that has changed. Although lefthanders still don't have every club available to them, they have most of what right-handers can get today. The best in woods, irons and putters are now available for us, so choosing what's right for you isn't as much of an issue as it once was. We all still hear from everyone that we're "standing on the wrong side of the ball," but when we hit our drives past theirs, the jokes quickly stop.

Now let's talk about golf course design. Most golf courses are designed to accommodate the slice of right-handed golfers. Doglegs usually curve from left to right. Since 90% of golfers are right-handed, and 90% of them slice the ball to the right, golf course architects design most of their doglegs to curve from left to right. This keeps the average right-hander in the fairway most of the time, and leads to a happy membership. If you are left-handed and can play a draw from left to right, you've got it made. These right-handed slicer holes are perfect for you. You can stand on the tee box and just cream it around the corner with power and accuracy because these holes match your ball flight. Start it up the left side and draw it around the corner. Boom.

The problem, however, is that if you're a lefty and you slice the ball, just like the majority of your right-handed counterparts, your ball is curving to the left, and the hole is curving to the right. Breaking 100 may be difficult if your ball is always in the left rough or fairway bunker. I promise that by the time you're finished with *On the Other Hand*, this won't be a problem. The chapters to come will teach you how to draw the ball naturally and start you on a lifetime of great golf.

But, before we begin, there is one, very important part of my career you need to know about. Several years ago I had the rare opportunity to head up the Ken Venturi Golf Training Center on Hilton Head Island, South Carolina. It was an extraordinary experience. Mr. Venturi is, without question, one of the great masters of the game and one of its greatest instructors. No one comes close to his advice on how to play your short game. And no one can hold a candle to the influence Mr. Venturi has had on contemporary golf, from the CBS press box to my lesson tee. That influence extends to this book, and I thank him. I will also refer to his wisdom throughout the book.

As you read through *On the Other Hand* and look at the pictures, I hope everything is easy to understand and that the information makes sense. You will notice a pattern in my approach to teaching. I start with the general and work my way to the specific. I like to talk about the fundamentals that I think create a good swing, what happens during a bad swing, and then how to correct it. Using every day movements, I try to simplify the complex action of swinging a golf club.

I always thought it odd that some books written by Tour pros ask you to do exactly what they do, where the reality of the situation is most of us can't swing like they do. Their natural talent, flexibility, and available time to hit balls are far different from most of us, and it is unreasonable to try and copy their swings.

I'm not prejudiced. For the right-handed golfers out there, this book can be of great benefit to you too. Simply change the left and right words (where have you heard that one), and when you're looking at the pictures, simply think you are looking into a mirror.

O.K. lefthanders, it's your turn!

Chapter One:
The 3 Fundamentals

Chapter One: The 3 Fundamentals

Before the actual instruction begins, I want you to understand a few things. I am not a famous golfer. I've never won the Masters or U.S. OPEN. Although I get more and more pros coming to me each year, I don't teach Greg Norman or Nick Faldo. What I have done is spent more than 20 years on the lesson tee, working in the trenches, watching tens of thousands of golfers just like you trying to hit a golf ball better, longer, and straighter. I have had great success in improving golfers like you and have shown them what they need to do to hit a successful golf shot. I have taken hundreds of golfers who were on the verge of quitting (especially left-handers) down to single digit handicaps and have gained insights into teaching the game of golf that can only be gained through experience.

During those years on the lesson tee, I have studied thousands of golf swings. I've watched my students and Tour professionals, and I've clipped every swing article that came across my desk that seemed interesting. I observed weekend golfers trying to line it out to the 300-yard marker at the driving range. And I pocketed those special, subtle differences between the left-handed golfer and the right-handed player.

When you see that many swings, you can't help but notice what average golfers tend to do and how their balls fly. You notice what the best golfers on the Tour do and how their balls fly differently from that of the novice player. You read what top golf teachers key on in their own instruction, and why they believe it is important.

Famous? No. A student and teacher of the greatest game in the world? That has been my pleasure. It has also been my goal to see if I could discover similarities in the swings of the game's greatest players. After all, if I was going to develop a swing of my own, imitating the best seemed only to make sense. Several years ago, I set off to find a swing model that I could base my own swing on and one I could successfully teach to my students, whether they swung from the left or right.

I studied every Tour pro's swing I could. Many examples I picked up from books or magazines, and countless others I examined when the Tour came to town. On a few occasions, I brought my video camera to the practice tee and taped the pros close up. I got just about every one of them, including Norman, Faldo, Couples, and Love. My current library consists of 92 Tour professionals. I watched their swings, frame by frame, on my VCR, stopping at key points along the way. I compared many of the "old guard" like Palmer, Hogan and Nelson (which came from printed material) to my tapes. I started discovering key points that molded my opinion of what made up a good golf swing. No two of these players had exactly the same swing, but there were some positions that most, if not all, had in common. And it didn't matter if the player swung from the left or right. The positions were the same.

In nearly 100 of the greatest players' swings, there seemed to be three positions they all shared. Not 100: **THREE.**

While there may have been a few dozen points in their swings that half of them did the same, those three magic positions always seemed to be there with every successful shot. I was shocked and surprised by this. The game suddenly appeared to be a whole lot easier to handle both as student and instructor. If I could develop a lesson plan to show other golfers these key moves and share with them what I had found, then maybe, just maybe this game wouldn't be so hard after all. That is how the *Three Fundamentals* were born.

I knew, of course, there were more than three pieces of information that a student needs to be shown, but now it seemed there were only **three big ones** that could make a tremendous difference. I would still have to get rid of a golfer's bad swing flaws, often a time-consuming effort for both teacher and student. I would also have to relate thoughts and ideas to the student about what he or she should feel during the swing, and explain what was happening to the club as they swung it. But now there were three very clear goals I wanted my students to achieve and positions I wanted them to get into.

Just three.

When I'm in the pro shop talking with a potential student, I make it a point to say, "If you can do three things, you can get very good at this game." It usually doesn't take the golfer long to make his first appointment. That commitment is one of the most rewarding parts of my job. I know that another golfer is on the road to improvement.

What was so odd about the study was that even the swings on the Tour that seemed unorthodox contained the Three Fundamentals. A Trevino, a Chi-Chi or a Ray Floyd did them as consistently as the textbook swings of an Elkington, Els or Woods. They may have arrived at them in different ways, but they sure did them. With this ammunition under my belt, I soon developed a teaching plan that could show my students what they needed to work on to become proficient, successful ball-strikers.

Because there are three fundamentals, I usually see a student three different times on the lesson tee. It takes me nearly an hour to show them each one. Then the student goes off and practices the first before I show the second. The fundamentals are not difficult things to do, but doing all of them at the same time is a bit overwhelming. The following chapters detail what the **big three** are and give you drills and checkpoints to ensure you are performing them properly.

The chapters on the short game also touch on positions that most of the Tour's finest players achieve, and show you why they are important in your own game. While I didn't see any techniques or positions in the short game that *all* the pros did, I must say that *most* of them did the same thing. Nicklaus putts nothing like Ben Crenshaw but they both share some similarities. They're both great putters and that's all you have to remember.

If your own pro teaches something different than what appears in this book, or your club champ disagrees with one of the fundamentals, I think that's fine. I don't have all the answers and welcome opinions of others. If you can stand on your head with your eyes closed and shoot par golf, then go with it. The information assembled in this book is taken from the game's greatest players, from what Venturi showed me, what Nelson and Hogan showed him, and from my own 35,000 plus lessons. These three fundamentals have always improved my own students' golf games and I think they are sound in their reasoning and presentation.

There are some things I may not agree with in some other instruction methods, and some pros may not agree with mine. That doesn't matter. As golf professionals, our single goal is to improve your game. Whatever approach works best for you is the one to use. It seems that every day I spend on the lesson tee I learn something new. It might be a new way to explain a technique, or maybe express a feeling the player should have during his swing. People grasp concepts differently, with one student liking one explanation and the next student another. My job is to give you the method that is best for you.

But please remember this. Fads come and go, not only in neckties but in golf instruction too. What's popular one year may not be the next. I have always remembered one of Venturi's quotes that definitely applies: "I always go back to the fundamentals. Without them, you have nothing."

Chapter Two:
The Address Position

Chapter Two: The Address Position

Before any instruction on the golf swing begins, the proper set-up must be understood. I have often said that you can have the best swing in the world, but if you're standing there incorrectly, you'll hit the ball incorrectly. Far too many golfers don't spend enough time working on their stance. It's a shame really, because it's the one part of the game that the average player can do as well as a Tour pro. Most of us will never swing back as much as Tiger Woods or have the swing speed of Fred Couples. But we can all *stand* there as well as they do. A senior player will never have the flexibility of a 25-year-old Tour professional, but he can look just as good at address!

But the address position is more than looks. It is the starting point of your swing and everything that happens in that swing is influenced by your stance. Think of shooting a rifle. You may have the best rifle money can buy but you won't hit your target if you're not aiming at it. Players get far too caught up in swinging the club and don't realize the swing itself stems from a solid starting position.

Understand, too, the address position is much more than just your aim. It encompasses your grip, posture, balance, weight distribution, distance from the ball, head position, arm position and alignment. Every one of these factors has a direct relation to how you swing the golf club. Each element must be present if you expect to hit a solid shot. I would say that at least 50% of all bad golf shots occur because of a poor set-up. Let me give you some examples to show you just

how the set-up influences the swing. We'll start with improper address positions because, unfortunately, you might recognize them more easily.

Poor Setup

Photo 1. This player slices the ball. No matter what he tries to do, his ball

Photo 1: This player slices the ball. No matter what he tries to do, his ball often fades to the left.

has a tendency to fade to the left. In his practice sessions on the range, he realizes the clubface is open at impact, causing his slice. While this is true, what the player should be asking himself is, "why is it open?" "Where is the problem starting?" It may very well be starting at his address. If we keep asking "why," then we can work our way back to the beginning.

A) The player slices the ball to the left. Why?

B) Realizes the clubface is open. Why?

C) The arms haven't rolled over. Why?

D) The upper body has swayed ahead of the ball, preventing the arm rotation. Why?

E) The player did not get behind the ball enough during the backswing. Why?

F) He did not have a full shoulder turn. Why?

At address, his head was in front of the ball, prohibiting the proper turn!

The player's clubface was open at impact because his head was not in the proper place during his set-up. It's interesting that all these other flaws happened because of the head. If the head were back where it belonged the golfer would have:

A) Turned better.

B) Been further behind the ball.

C) Not gotten ahead of the ball on the downswing.

D) Been able to roll his arms over.

E) Squared up the clubface.

F) Hit a straight shot.

The improper set-up caused the bad shot.

Over the Top

Here's another scenario.

Photo 2. This player pulls his shots to the right. Why?

A) The clubface is closed at impact. Why?

B) He's coming over the top. Why?

C) The left shoulder is moving outside of the right. Why?

D) The shoulders were open at address. Why?

Photo 2: This player often pulls his shots to the right.

The player was not tilted back correctly at address.

The player came over the top (arms moving down before the legs) because at address, his left arm was too far away from his body, which forced his shoulders to be open.

There are dozens of examples I could give, but just these two should make you realize how important the proper address position is. Remember that the problem always goes back to the stance, and that you can stand there like a pro.

Breaking Down the Address Position

The Grip.

Your only attachment to the golf club is your grip. Many of golf's finest players and best teachers feel that there is no other part of this game that is more important. I share those feelings. A perfect swing with a poor grip will generally produce shots that are less than desirable. No matter how well a golfer turns back away from the ball or how powerfully his legs drive, the accuracy of the shot will be inconsistent if the grip is not solid.

However, and this is a big however, there have been some Tour players who have achieved great success with less than perfect grips. It's an element of the golf swing that can have many variations and still be considered effective. Fred Couples, Paul Azinger, and David Duval have very strong grips (the hands are turned more to the right for righthanders). Other notable players have the hands in a weak position (the hands are more passive during the swing). Some players use an overlapping or Vardon grip. Some use the interlocking grip, while still others (although not very many) use a ten-finger or baseball grip.

There are a variety of acceptable grips in this game because there are a variety of ways the golf club can be swung. A weak or slow swing may require a stronger grip, while a fast, powerful swing that uses the body very well, may need a grip that is a bit weaker. There is not one correct grip for everyone, but there is a correct grip for you. It would be a mistake for me to say, "This is the way to hold your club, period, no exceptions!" A golf professional cannot tell you what is best for you unless he sees you swing. Just because Nicklaus holds his club a certain way doesn't mean that's the best way for you. Jack's grip is beautiful, but it's Jack's, not yours.

The pictures at the end of this section show you several variations on the grip, how your hands should be placed on the club, and what it should feel like. Through experience, I have found that it's easier to learn the rest of the set-up if you first do it with your own grip, then learn a new one later. A new grip may feel so unusual to you that it takes your attention away from learning the other fundamentals of the stance and swing, so let's keep the grip change until the end.

Alignment

Without an ounce of doubt I would say 90% of golfers don't aim properly. Lefthanders aim off to the left, while righthanders align to the right. It is one of the hardest qualities to get right in your golf game. Most of us wouldn't intentionally aim poorly, but we all do. While this may seem obvious, you'll hit it off line if you're aiming off line. We all swear that we're aiming correctly and are shocked when we are shown how far off we really are.

Why is aiming so difficult?

After much research and thousands of lessons, I can tell you this. Every human being has one eye that is stronger than the other eye. Known as your dominant eye, it's the eye that is actually registering with the brain. You see the ball with both eyes but your brain sees it with only one. More than ninety-five percent of left-handed players are left-eye dominant. The same percentage of righthanders are right eye dominant. When a left-handed golfer is addressing the golf ball, the brain sees the ball through the left eye. Since the left eye is behind the ball and looks at it from an angled position, aiming off to the left looks straight. When I stand behind my students and ask them to aim at a specific flagstick on the range, they usually are pointing 10-40 yards off to the left. When I lay a club down at their feet across their toe line and pull them back where I'm standing, they are shocked. They usually say, "I could have sworn I was aiming at the pin." That last shot you pushed 20 yards left? That was where you were probably aiming. You actually hit the ball straight!

Aiming to the left will not only get you in trouble and add strokes to your score, but can lead to more and more errors. If you aim off to the left and don't know it, you'll either hit the ball there, or your subconscious brain will try to correct your swing. Then you pull the ball to attempt to get it back on line. If your brain realizes your alignment is too far left, then somewhere in your downswing, it tells your body to pull the ball back on line. You may pull it just enough to hit the ball straight sometimes, but "sometimes" is not a word we use. You want to hit it straight consistently. If you over-compensate, you'll hit a pull or hook to the right. Now you're really confused because the ball never seems to go to the same place twice in a row.

The real crime is that most average players, when faced with inconsistency like this, immediately start questioning their swing. They ask, "What am I doing wrong?" In many cases, nothing. They swing incorrectly because they're aiming incorrectly. The only way to hit your target if you're aiming 20 yards to the left is to pull the ball 20 yards to the right. It ends up on the green and you think you've figured out what the problem is. But on the next swing you don't get the pull happening and there it goes, off to the left, into the woods again.

Why not just aim correctly and have one less thing to worry about?

Photo 3 shows the correct way to align yourself to the golf ball. The word square or parallel is most impor-

Photo 3: Here is the correct way to align yourself to the golf ball.

tant. Line A shows a straight line drawn from your ball to the target. This is known as your target line and is the path the ball will fly on. You don't stand on this line when you address the ball because you would be standing directly on top of the ball! You stand over to the side of the ball. You've probably heard or seen the "train track" image. Believe me, it works. The ball flies down the outside rail (**A**) and you stand on the inside rail (**B**). Your feet are parallel to the target line, so in reality your body is aiming right of the target. Make sure you understand this. You stand to the side of the ball, so 200 yards down the fairway your body is right of the target. It has to be.

Most golfers, on purpose or by accident, aim their body right at the target, which causes the ball to fly on a line that is off to the left. Again, the only way your body could point at the target is if you were standing on the same line the ball flies on. The train track diagram should help show you this clearly.

To help you line up properly on the driving range, simply lay an extra club on the ground between you and the ball that is parallel to the target line. Your toes should be parallel to this club. Ball after ball, day after day, and year after year, if you hit range balls with this club at your feet, and leave it there, you'll get used to standing correctly. If this club is not there, you may be wasting your time because your alignment may be off. There is no reason to work on your golf swing if your stance is wrong.

In my own lessons, I am constantly amazed how much better, straighter, and further my students hit the ball when I simply get them aiming better. Most of us could understand why the accuracy would improve, but the increase of distance may be confusing.

Here's why. When a golfer aims squarely, the brain realizes it and tells the golfer, "Hey, you can go ahead and free wheel through this, you don't have to steer it anymore." The body can have a full, powerful release through the ball, which generally increases the clubhead speed. When the alignment is off, the body is afraid to swing all out, fearing an off-line shot, and tries to steer the ball. Aiming to the left forces the golfer to pull the swing to the right and usually results in a "chicken wing" with the right arm. The arms pull up and wrap around the body tightly rather than extending long and full toward the target.

Think of a home run hitter coming to the plate in baseball. The pitcher does not want to throw a high outside pitch to this guy. The batter will hit it out of the park. The term, "getting your arms extended out over the plate" is frequently heard from the batting coach. This gives the batter the maximum extension with his arms, which creates much of the power. To throw to this batter, the pitcher is instructed to pitch him inside, or "jam him." The batter cannot get his arms extended at all and pulls the arms in and around his body, hitting the ball off the handle.

Ben Hogan said to throw your arms away from you on the downswing. This is much the same thought as extending the arms out over the plate. The golfer that aims to the left cannot do this or the ball will fly out way left. The player that aims correctly (parallel) can swing the arms out, and achieve maximum power. Once again the set-up, and in this case the alignment, greatly influences the golfer's swing.

Ball Position

There are two schools of thought on ball position, or where the ball is in relation to your feet.

The first method is to keep the ball position constant when you change clubs. In other words, the woods and irons are all played off the same position, usually just inside the front heel. This lets the golfer set-up with the ball consistently in the same place and is the method use by many top Tour professionals.

The second method is to move the ball every time you change clubs. This is the method I use with my own students and is what I believe most amateur golfers should use. I personally have a hard time believing that a driver and a pitching wedge are going to hit the ground at the same spot. Just holding them up side-by-side shows you that the driver is quite a bit longer and has a different lie (the angle the shaft goes into the head). For most golfers, that tells me the clubs would hit the ground at a different point. Modern drivers are 44 or 45 inches long. Most pitching wedges measure in at 36 1/2 inches. In my mind, these clubs do not hit the ground at the same point. The driver also swings on a shallower plane than the pitching wedge, which swings more up and down, causing the wedge to hit the ground earlier.

The reasoning behind the pros playing and keeping the ball forward is this. Tour professionals generate tremendous power in their swing and use their legs quite effectively. After they complete their backswing, their legs and body turn powerfully through on the downswing. They can get the legs and body further forward, moving toward the target faster and better than the average player. The bottom of their swing, or center of gravity, moves closer to the front heel than the average player. Their club reaches the low spot in the swing (where it hits the ground) off the front heel. Their weight is more on the front leg at impact than the average player, causing their club to hit into the turf in a spot closer to the front heel.

The average player does not move his legs as fast as this, and his club tends to hit the ground further back in his stance. Common sense should tell us if your club hits the low spot (center of gravity) in the middle of your stance, that's where the ball should be. I would say 98% of my students have better success moving the ball position forward and backward. If you swing like Jack Nicklaus, you may want to play the ball in a forward position. But if you're like the rest of us, try moving it. Changing the position of the ball will lead to crisper contact. So where do you put it?

Photo 4: To check ball position, form a cross.

Where to Start

Your 7 iron is your magic club. This is the club that should have the ball in the direct center of your stance. After addressing your shot, draw your eyes from the ball back toward your feet. Make sure the ball is in the middle of your stance. When you're on the range, take an extra club out of your bag and lay it across the other one that should be showing you your alignment. Form a cross. A ball teed right off the grip is now in a position to be easily checked. *Photo 4.*

When you change clubs, move the ball position. How much? Take a 6 iron out of your bag and hold it next to your 7. If your clubs are "normal," the 6 iron is one half inch longer than the 7. Every club is made in one half inch increments. The 4 is longer than the 5, the 5 is longer than the 6, and so on. The 7 is in the middle of the stance. When you go to your 6 iron, you'll move the ball one half-inch forward (to the right). It moves one half inch because the club lengthens by one half inch. Your 5 would require another one half-inch move until, all the way down to the driver, your ball is off your front heel. Your 8 iron moves one half-inch back of center and your 9 is one half-inch more than this. This really simplifies where your ball position needs to be and gives you an accurate way of measuring it.

There is another reason I believe your ball position should change. As the length of your club changes, so does the lie. A complete description of what "lie" is will be discussed in Chapter 11 (clubfitting), but for now, know this. The shaft goes into the head of the club at a certain angle, and this angle changes when the length of the club changes. The wedges are the shortest shafted clubs in the bag, and have the most upright lie. The handle, or grip end of these clubs is higher off the ground, or more toward a 90 degree angle. A long club, like a driver, has a flatter lie, with the grip lower or closer to the ground. See *Photo 5.*

The longer or flatter a club is, the shallower it swings up and down. The club goes back lower to the ground on the backswing and comes in lower on the downswing. The idea of an air-

Photo 5: Check the "lie" of the club.

plane landing is helpful. The plane comes in and gradually gets lower and lower to the ground on its approach. It doesn't just fall straight down. This "shallow" approach with the long club makes the clubhead hit the ground nearer to your front heel. A short club, like a pitching wedge, has a very upright lie. This promotes a more up and down swing. The club goes back higher and steeper on the backswing, then quite naturally swings down steeper, more like a helicopter landing. This steep approach tends to hit the ground sooner, or closer to your back foot. Understanding how lengths and lies affect your swing aids you in understanding ball position.

To recap, with a 7 iron, play the ball in the middle of your stance and move it one half-inch per club. The lower numbered irons move toward the right heel, and the higher numbers toward the left.

If the ball is not in the proper position, a variety of bad shots may result. There is always a chance that your swing was not good on that particular effort. But before you start picking your swing apart, make sure the ball position was not at fault. The following is a list of what may happen to your shot if the ball is in the wrong position.

If the ball is too far forward.

If the golf ball is too close to the right heel for the club you are hitting, you may:

A) Top it.
B) Hit it fat.
C) Pull it.
D) Slice it.

The topped or thin shot occurs because of this. From the top of your swing, the club begins moving down toward the ball. The clubhead gets lower and lower as it approaches the ball. If you were hitting a 7 iron, the clubhead would reach the low spot (where it hits the ground) in the middle of your stance. That's where the ball should be. The club then starts to rise back up as you advance into your follow through. Because the club starts swinging up, it strikes the ball on the top, above its equator, and the shot is topped. In other words, by the time the club reached the ball, it was already starting its upswing. It's kind of hard to hit down and take a divot when your club is going up!

Having the ball too far forward may also result in a fat shot. Your club swings down and hits into the turf at its designated spot. Using the 7 iron as our model, this spot is again in the middle. If the ball is too far forward, the club only hits the ground instead of the ball. Ouch.

Positioning the ball too far forward can also result in a pull. If the 7 iron squares up with the clubface looking at the target, when it's in the middle of your stance, by the time the club reaches the ball the face is starting to

close. If you were playing the ball off your right heel, (which is three inches too far forward for a 7 iron), the face of the club will be very closed by the time it strikes the ball. The slice happens for much the same reason. By the time the club strikes the ball, it "saws" across it, imparting a "slice spin."

Even with a perfect swing, you can't hit the ball from this position.

If the ball is too far back.

If the ball is too far back in the stance, you may:

A) Top it.
B) Push it.
C) Shank it.
D) Slice it.

The topped shot happens because the club, on its downswing, has not reached its low spot yet, so it strikes the ball on top. Where the 7 iron would reach the ground in the middle of your stance, it's still a few inches off the ground as it passes your left toe. Playing the ball even two inches too far back may result in a terribly topped shot or even a whiff.

The ball may also push, or slice, off to the left because the clubface has not squared up yet. If the ball was in the correct position, the clubface would have just a bit more time to square up. The face of the club is still pointing to the left (open) when it hits a ball that is played too far back.

The shank happens for much the same reason. With the ball too far back, the clubface won't have time to square up and it gets to the ball before it should. The ball is hit off the hosel (where the shaft meets the head) of the golf club. It's like a push, but much worse. If the ball was where it should be, the clubface would square up and hit the ball in the middle of the club-face or sweet spot.

You can see that the position of the ball is crucial in good shot making. A good swing combined with a bad ball position will always result in a bad shot.

Weight Distribution

What we are discussing here is how your weight is distributed between your feet on a regular "full" swing. This will change during your short game, which will be covered in later chapters. The balance your body has during the swing is greatly influenced by where your weight is during the set-up.

For most standard, full swing shots you should have half your weight on the left foot, and half on the right. Basically, it's just how your body would be when you're standing still, talking with someone. Your feet should be at shoulder's width.

On higher lofted clubs, like a 7,8,9, and wedge, have about 15% more weight on the front foot. This sets your weight forward, which encourages a descending blow to the ball. Because these clubs are short, the swing does-n't take as long to happen as with longer clubs. Your body doesn't have as much time to turn out of the way on the downswing as it does on a driver. Putting a bit more weight on the front helps you strike the ball better.

On your woods, try having 10% to 15% more weight on the left leg. This helps get your head and upper body back a bit further, and encourages a more sweeping swing, which your long irons and woods require.

Of much more importance though, is where your weight is from front to back, or from heels to toes. This ele-ment is most important to maintaining your balance. I like the weight to be toward the heels -- not totally on the heels but toward them. Here is a great checkpoint. When you're at your address position and holding your club, you should be able to wiggle your toes. When your toes can wiggle up and down, you know you have just enough weight back. If your weight is too far forward, you can't wiggle your toes.

Weight too far forward.

Some bad shots that can happen if your weight is too much on the toes are:

A) A shank.
B) A fat shot.
C) A thin shot.
D) A pull.

You "shank" a shot when you strike the ball on the neck of the club or the hosel. This happens for a simple reason. If you swing back and your weight moves out toward the toes, your body also leans forward with your head moving out toward the ball. When your body goes forward, so does the club. The head of the club is pushed out an inch or two, which makes it strike the ball on the hosel. Keeping the weight back reduces this possibility.

The fat shot may also show its ugly self. If your body leans forward and your head lowers on your backswing, you are now lower than you were at your address. If everything has moved down, the clubhead hits down into the ground lower and earlier than it should. That is, you hit it FAT!

The thin or topped shot is also a result of dipping down. During your backswing, your body realizes it has dipped forward. To stop the fat shot from happening, your body lifts up during the downswing and boom, you top it.

A pulled shot may well be the most common bad shot that occurs when your weight goes toward your toes. If your weight starts moving out toward your toes too much, your body feels like it is falling over. At the top of your swing your brain tells you that you're falling down. To stop this falling feeling, your arms swing the club around your body to the right and your ball starts right. Think of it this way. At the top of your swing, your head is dropping forward toward the ball, making you feel like you are falling on your face. To stop it, your body lifts up and pulls you and your club around your body, which causes the pull or pull slice.

Keeping some weight back, toward the heels, lets your body swing powerfully through the ball without fear of losing balance. In his book, *The Venturi Analysis*, Ken Venturi says this about Byron Nelson. "To get comfortably closer to the ball, and maintain good balance, Byron set his weight back toward his heels."

Ben Hogan's *Five Lessons Book* says to "wiggle the toes." Think of the movement of a prizefighter. When the boxer wants to hit you really hard, he rears back and gets his weight toward his heels. From this powerful position he can explode forward, moving out onto his toes. Having your weight toward the heels lets you move out onto your toes during the swing. How can you get any power being on your toes at the top of the swing -- or any movement? Mike Tyson can only hit

you so hard if he's hitting you from his toes.

Distance from the Ball

How far should you stand from the ball? Are you too close or too far away? How can you know for sure that you are standing the proper distance from the ball? Here is an easy

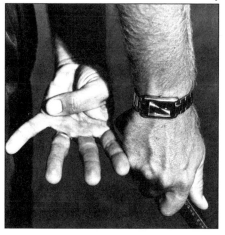

Photo 6: The four-finger spread.

drill.

Take your stance to the ball holding any club. Keep your right hand holding the club, but take your left hand off. Hold your left hand up in front of you with the palm up. Put your thumb across. Spread your four fingers. See *Photo 6*. This four-finger spread should fit between your right thigh and the end of your grip. A gap of four spread fingers should fit neatly between the butt end of your club and the inside of your right leg. This will hold true for all your clubs for all standard, full swing shots. Chipping and putting are, of course, different.

Using this measure as a checkpoint ensures that you are the proper distance at address. Most average golfers stand too far from the ball, which causes poor balance. It would be very easy to end up on your toes if you stand too far from the ball. You read what could happen in that instance. Make sure your distance from the ball doesn't create another problem.

Being too close to the ball can also create problems. If your club is too close to you, there may not be enough room for it to pass you when you swing down. This forces the club out too much, resulting in a shank again. You need to give the club some room to come down, so make sure the 4-finger gap is there.

Posture

Your ball position, your distance from the ball, and weight distribution

Photo 7: The correct "bowing motion.

are all major factors in your posture. To me, posture means the angle and position your upper body is in relation to your lower body. You don't want to

Photo 8: The "slouch."

stand up perfectly straight, nor do you want to be all bent over.

I like the body to be in what I can best describe as a "bowing motion." As *Photo 7* illustrates, this golfer is bending at the waist approximately 30 degrees. When the knees flex and the weight goes back toward the heels, a strong posture position is created.

The golfer in *Photo 8* is all slouched over and looks tired. This starting position will do nothing but lead to a bad swing. Hogan said, "Your rear end sort of sticks out like you're sitting on a spectator's stick." Some pros like to see a straight back. These are all good ideas. A word of caution: poor posture can also lead to an injury, especially to the lower back. If you are slouched over, your back is in a position that may twist it, causing an injury.

Having your knees slightly flexed

at address (an inch or two) takes pressure off your lower back and puts your legs in an athletic position. The legs are now like two springs that can help add power during your swing. Straight, stiff legs are dead legs that cannot contribute to the swing. When a sprinter is getting ready for a 100-meter run, his body is down low to the ground, with the knees bent. When the gun sounds, he can spring up with tremendous power. Imagine him just standing there with straight legs. He couldn't jump off the line with any authority. Your body should feel "ready," like it's ready for action, just like the sprinter.

Put your backside two inches outside of your heels. You now have a counterweight to keep you from falling forward. I like to think of a construction crane. The long arm of the crane would fall over forward if not for the big weight back down on the ground. Your head, chest, arms and club are trying to pull you over the ball, so your backside needs to counter this by sticking out.

The Tilt: The Magic Position in Your Stance.

If there is one element of the address position that far outweighs the others in order of importance, it's what I call "the tilt." Not only does your upper body need to be parallel to the target line (the "outside rail"), but it also needs to be angled correctly.

The left side of your body, and your left shoulder and arm, must be lower than your right.

This is something that is not only important, but has to happen. Unless you swing cross-handed on your full swings, which is highly unlikely, your left hand is lower than your right. If your left hand is lower than your right, then your left shoulder must be lower than your right shoulder. When addressing the ball correctly, your upper body, or spine, tilts back slightly, lowering your left shoulder. Your spine is angled some 10 degrees to the left.

When you do this, your head moves back to the left as well, positioning it behind the ball. Your right ear is lined up with the golf ball. Your head will be farther behind the ball on a drive because you play the ball on a drive farther forward.

Your nose is about 5 inches behind the ball. All this happens when you "tilt." Most amateurs line up with their nose directly over the ball or worse,

Photo 9: The proper "tilt."

have their head in front of the ball. They think this is correct and try to stand there with their shoulders per-

Photo 10: An incorrect "tilt."

Photo 11: Relationship of left elbow to left hip.

fectly level to the ground. Wrong, wrong, wrong!

In all my lessons, this is one correction I have to make with literally every student. Even a two handicapper doesn't do this correctly. In my opinion it is the #1 mistake average players make. What is worse, they have no idea that they should be tilted.

Photo 9 illustrates the proper tilting motion and clearly shows where the head is in relation to the ball. This golfer is in a position to hit a good shot right from the outset.

Photo 10 shows how most golfers address the ball with the head out of position and an incorrect shoulder tilt.

When you are in the correct tilted position, there is another important factor that happens. Your right arm should be two inches above your left arm. The right arm is further away from your body than your left arm is.

Your left arm and elbow are closer to your body than your right arm is. The left elbow is very close to the left hip. *Photo # 11* shows the correct position. If you were standing in front of me, I should be able to put a golf club through your arms, with the right arm over the club and the left arm under it. The only possible way to have your left hand below your right, and keep your left arm inward of the right arm, is if you tilt.

During my first lesson with new students, this is one of the first items I show them and I am always astounded how much better they hit the ball simply by making this correction. Before doing anything on their swing, I get them to tilt properly and BAM! They hit the ball like they never have before. Ninety percent of them arrive with a slice, and 99% of them draw the ball with this simple correction. So will you!

Why the Tilt Is So Important.

Other than simply being correct, looking better, and feeling more powerful, the tilt has a dramatic effect on the way you hit the ball. The following lists what happens to your swing when you tilt and when you don't, and what bad shots may occur as a result. We discussed getting to the root of a problem when you asked yourself "why," and laid out how so many swing problems actually start at your address position. As you will see, many of your swing flaws are caused by not having the tilt.

A) Lack of power in your swing.

When your body is not tilted back, your head stays in front of the ball. Turning your shoulders back behind the ball on the backswing is crucial in attaining power. Fundamental #1 will cover this in depth later on. It is virtually impossible to get any measurable shoulder turn if your head stays in front of the ball. With the tilt, your head is behind the ball at your address position, which allows your shoulders to turn a great deal. The golfer whose head is in front of the ball can only swing back with his arms, which can never generate the power that the whole body can.

Imagine trying to throw a baseball, keeping your head forward. You couldn't turn back nearly enough to throw the ball any distance. If you swing back with just your arms, your weight stays forward on your front foot. When you swing down, your weight may actually go back. You end up on your left foot falling over backwards. This is commonly referred to as a reverse weight shift and is prevalent in many high handicappers' swings. It doesn't make much sense to try to hit the ball in one direction and fall over in the other direction. With your upper body tilted back and your head behind the ball, your weight shifts onto your left leg. From here, a powerful transfer of weight over to your right side naturally occurs, gaining you distance you may not be accustomed to. Natural power!

B) A Slice.

With your head in front of the ball in a non-tilted position, you may slice the ball. As you just read, your shoulders cannot turn back when your head is in front of the golf ball. If your shoulders don't turn back enough, you never get your body behind the ball. Since you're not behind the ball on your backswing, you move ahead of the ball on your downswing and the ball slices. The face of your club can't square up as it hits the ball because your upper body has moved ahead of its center. *Photo 12* shows this. The golfer has moved her upper body ahead of where it was at address, which does not allow the club to square up until after it has hit the ball. The clubface is still open at impact. This could either push or slice the ball.

Think of opening and closing a door. If the door opens three feet on the backswing, then closes three feet on the downswing, it's square. If the door opens only two feet on the backswing then tries to close three feet, it's still open. It would not shut squarely. This lack of turn is the major reason I see students slice the ball. It's really a shame, because it's so easy to correct. Simply getting the tilt moves your head back and lets your shoulders turn enough on the backswing, which squares up the clubface at impact.

The slice is also generated from this position because the club cannot go back on the proper line. With your head too far forward, and your left arm not tucked in, you're in an "open" position with your shoulders, which causes the club to move out from you on the backswing. This, in turn, causes the downswing to do the reverse, to move in, cutting across the ball and producing a slice.

Photo 12: The clubface is still open at impact.

C) A Pull.

The lack of a tilt can make the ball start to the right of your target. Similar to the last problem, your shoulders are open (pointing to the right) at address because the left arm is outside of the right. When you swing the club back, it starts going outside the target line. On the downswing, it's moving too far inside or right, and a pull results. If your shoulders are aiming to the right at address, the club swings that way as it strikes the ball. You couldn't square your shoulders at address because you didn't tilt.

Depending on the position of your clubface at impact, you either hit a straight pull, or a pull-slice if the clubface if open. If the face of the club happened to close, which is the rarity, you would hit a pull-hook. That's never fun. The ball starts right and curves more right.

D) A Fat Shot.

Once again the lack of a tilt can cause another ugly shot. With no tilt, your arms pick the club up too steeply on your backswing. Because you swing up too steeply on the backswing, you swing down too steeply on the downswing and stick the club into the ground several inches behind the ball. With an insufficient shoulder turn, the arms take over and cause a swing that is far too upright. Up, down, fat! The fat shot is almost guaranteed right when you start if you don't tilt the spine back at address. The reverse weight shift that happens on the weak shot also makes the club come down behind the ball because the weight is moving back, toward the left foot, instead of forward toward the target.

E) The Thin or Topped Shot.

If your club doesn't stick into the ground three inches behind the ball, it starts climbing back up into your follow through. The club reaches the low spot too far back from your center of gravity, then starts going up. It's rather difficult to hit down on the ball when your club is moving up. The lack of tilt, which caused the head to be in front of the ball, hindered the shoulder-turn on the backswing. The arms swung up too steeply on the backswing and come down too steeply on the downswing. Immediately after reaching the low spot where it usually sticks into the ground, the club swings up sharply. There's your thin shot.

What explanations A through E show is the importance of the tilt. Getting this one element of your address position right can eliminate so many of golf's common swing problems. You don't have to be a world-class athlete to stand correctly, and the improvements that result are stunning.

Summary of Address Position

A)   Stand parallel to the target line. Laying a club at your feet is helpful.

B)   Position the ball in the middle of your stance with a 7 iron. Place a club across the other club at a 90 degree angle to form a cross. Position the ball off the end of this club, then move the ball position one half inch per club.

C)   Weight distribution. On all standard full swings, half your weight should be on your left foot and half on your right. For your 8,9, and wedges, put about 10-15% more on the front foot. On your woods have 10-15% more weight on the back foot.

D)   Have your weight toward your heels. Your toes should be able to wiggle. Knees are slightly flexed.

E)   Your distance from the ball? Four spread fingers should fit between the end of your grip to your right thigh.

F)   Tilt your spine away from the target. Your left hand is lower than your right hand. Your right ear should be lined up on the ball. Your head should be behind the ball. Your left arm is close to your left hip and the right arm is two inches outward of your left, or further away from your body.

G)   Your upper body should also be angled over by 30 degrees. Keep a nice straight back and don't slouch your shoulders.

The Grip

Remember: your only attachment to the golf club is your grip. Your hands must hold the club in a way that will return it squarely to the golf ball. The grip must be able to release the

Photo 13: The Baseball or Ten Finger Grip. Good for younger players and seniors with limited hand and arm strength.

club powerfully into the back of the ball, with a high degree of accuracy.

There are basically three acceptable ways to grip your club. However, there are dozens of variations of these three. The following sections show you what they are and offer suggestions about how to determine which grip is best for you.

The Ten Finger Grip

As the name suggests, all ten of your fingers are holding the golf club much the way you would grip a baseball bat. *Photo 13* is the grip style that is least preferred among golf professionals. The ten-finger grip tends to make your hands work separately from each other. It also makes the left hand feel too strong. If you're not careful, the left hand may overtake the right on your downswing and you will hook your shot. Most left-handed golfers are left-handed in every other activity. Their left hand is stronger than their right. This dominant left hand tries to overtake the right and rolls over too early at impact. This early roll either hooks the ball or simply pulls it right. The hands may also separate somewhere during the swing, which can cause many more problems.

However, the ten-finger grip does work well with some golfers. A junior player whose hand and arm strength has not yet developed may achieve success with this method. A senior golfer that has lost some of his arm strength may also feel more comfortable gripping like this. Either through age, injury, or a medical problem like arthritis, a senior may find he has a hard time hanging onto the club with any other style of grip. Some ladies are also comfortable with all ten fingers holding the club because their hands and wrists are not that strong.

Arm strength and swing speed are also factors that may steer you toward using the ten finger or baseball grip. It's the grip very few Tour professionals use, but it's not wrong.

Photo 14: The Interlocking Grip.

The Interlocking Grip

As the name indicates, your hands are locked together with your right forefinger and left small finger. See *Photo 14*. A large number of golf professionals use this grip, as do half of all amateur players.

Start by placing all ten fingers on the grip like the baseball grip. Now hold the club up in front of you. Take your right index finger off the club, then your left pinky. Now, link them together. Your hands are molded together and work as one unit, instead of working separately. Rather than two hands fighting each other for control, they are now working in harmony.

I would say 50% of golfers use this grip. The percentage is much higher if you include just women golfers. The interlocking style feels very comfortable for people with smaller hands. Of

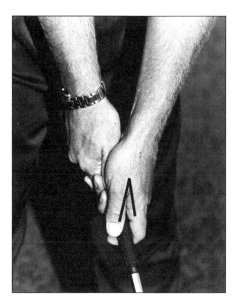

Photo 15: Forming a "V."

course, not all these golfers have small hands, but the vast majority do. If your hands are on the small side, this is probably the grip for you. The inter-locking method lets the club swing freely during the swing. Men with smaller hands may also like this style.

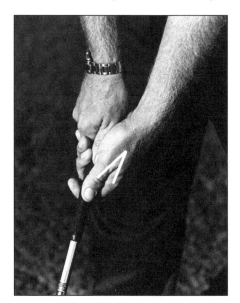

Photo 16: Too strong.

Jack Nicklaus has very small hands and has always gripped the club like this. Tiger Woods also uses this grip.

As far as the positioning of the hands, look at *Photo 15*. Where your thumbs touch the index fingers, they

Photo 17: "Weak Grip."

form a V. The Vs of both hands should point toward your left shoulder. This puts your hands in what is called a neutral position. This is how they would lay on the golf club if you clapped your hands together, then stuck a club in between them. The neutral positioning of your hands lets the club swing down and through the golf ball in a natural motion, squaring the clubface up at impact.

If both of your hands were turned too much to the left (*Photo 16*), it would make your hands too strong. When the back of your right hand is facing the sky it may roll over too much as you hit the ball and close the clubface drastically, causing a hook.

If the back of your right hand faces the target too much (*Photo 17*), the clubface may stay open on your downswing and a slice could occur. This is called a weak grip because during the downswing the hands do less than they should. They don't roll over at all and the clubface stays open through impact.

There are always exceptions to the rule, but generally these grip positions will dictate ball flight. Moving one hand or the other can dramatically influence this, so spend some time on the range trying out different grips. Your grip may also change over time, as your swing improves. A golfer that starts to swing with more power over the years may have to change his grip to match up with his new swing. As a

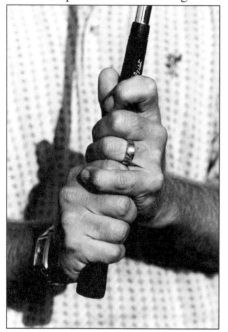

Photo 18: The "Vardon Grip."

senior loses some of his power over time, a stronger grip may be necessary.

The same rules apply to the overlapping grip described below.

The Overlapping Grip
This grip, also known as the Vardon Grip, is far and away the most popular with golf professionals and is the preference with average players. Developed by Harry Vardon at the start of the century, it quickly became the most used style in golf.

Similar to the interlocking grip, the Vardon links your two hands together but in a different way. Instead of the fingers interlocking with each other, the left pinky simply goes over the right index finger and nestles down in the crack. Photo 18 clearly shows this. Nine of your fingers are on the grip and your left pinky is over the others. People with average to large size hands tend to prefer this grip style. There are plenty of women and children who also use this method because it is more comfortable for them. Whatever feels and works best for you is the one to go with. Again, have your 'V's pointing more or less up your left arm. The hands are locked together, but are again in a neutral position.

How Tight?
The final word on the grip is the how tight you hold the club. Your grip pressure should be quite light and relaxed. The club should feel like it's going to fall out of your hands. If you squeeze the club too tightly, your hands and arms will have excessive tension and may reduce the smoothness in your swing. One of the best analogies I've ever heard is of holding a towel that is soaking wet. You should hold the towel tightly enough so you don't drop it, but you shouldn't squeeze any water out of it.

You hands will naturally firm up their grip during the swing, so don't be afraid of the club flying out of your hands.

Chapter Three:
Fundamental One: "The Triangle"

Chapter 3: Fundamental One

Chapter One touched on the 3 Fundamentals. To refresh your memory, there were three points in the Tour pros' swings that they all seemed to do identically. Fundamental One is the first of the "big three" and may very well be the most important. In my experience, it's the one part of the golf swing that I spend the most time on with my students. Fundamental One sets up the whole swing correctly. Without it, your swing will be a struggle.

Breaking Down Fundamental One

The first big move in the golf swing is how you swing the club from the address position back to waist high. This first move, back away from the ball, is crucial to your success in making a good swing. If you start your swing back correctly, it can only lead to the rest of the swing being solid. Where your club arrives at the top of the swing will be dictated by how it begins the backswing. How your club comes down into the ball will also be controlled by this first initial move back away from the ball.

I think my slingshot analogy is helpful. If you pull the rubber band back correctly it will snap through the frame correctly, launching your pebble at your target. Pull it back straight and it shoots through straight. If you pulled the rubber band back incorrectly, you would never know where your pebble was going to land or even whether it would make it through the sling shot frame! The book, *The Search for the Perfect Swing* says, "It thus seems certain that the key move in getting to the correct top-of-backswing position is

the first foot or so of the backswing. If this is achieved, the rest of the backswing will tend to follow naturally."

We will start by calling Fundamental One, The Triangle, because, at the address position, your arms and chest form a triangle. It's

Photo 19: "The Triangle."

upside down and tilted some, but it's still a triangle. (See *Photo 19*.)

Stick the end of the grip up under your chest with your arms extended down straight. From this position it's very easy to see the shape. There are several key factors the triangle shows us.

Our first goal is to turn the triangle back to waist high without breaking it. (*Photo 20*.) The triangle is there at address and is still there at waist high on your backswing. When you return back to the impact position, the trian-

Photo 20: Bring "The Triangle" back without breaking it

gle is there and continues to be there until waist high on your follow through. From waist high back to waist high through, you maintain your

Photo 21: Up on left toe.

triangle. Notice when you're in the follow through position, you should be up on your left toe. (*Photo 21*.)

The second item to notice is that the buttons on your shirt or the "V"

that your collar forms, points down at the head of your club. When you turn the triangle back to waist high, your

Photo 22: "V" still points to the head of the club.

"V" should still point at the head of the club. (*Photo 22*.) In other words, the middle of your chest points at the club at the address position, and follows it as the club swings back and through to waist high. When your "V" points at the clubhead in the waist high follow through position, you are again up on your left toe.

What these two moves do is turn your shoulders.

When the triangle moves back together with your "V," your shoulders turn. They turn right from the start and they turn 90 degrees. Your right shoulder is starting to turn behind the ball. At address, the outside edge of your right shoulder is in front of the ball and is closer to the target than the ball is. When you turn your triangle back to waist high the shoulder moves behind the ball. The ball is now closer to the target than your shoulder is. Your back is now facing the target.

This first move back with your shoulders does one very important thing. It gets your body involved. Your body moves the club back when the shoulders turn. Think about these numbers for a moment. I weigh 170 pounds. My arms weigh about 10 pounds. My golf club weighs one pound. You're not going to get much power if you only use the club. Your arms are not going to do much either. Your body gives you all the power because it's so big. Even a smaller person who only weighs 100 pounds still weighs a heck of a lot more than a golf ball.

A 170-pound man weighs nearly 2,000 times more than a golf ball. You don't have to swing hard to hit it far. You simply have to use your weight correctly. Turning your triangle back does this for you. From the moment you put your swing into motion, your body is moving and is heavily involved. A 90-degree shoulder turn is what most of us should strive for, with the right shoulder getting three or four inches behind the ball. As you get better, these numbers may increase some, eventually getting into the Tiger Woods neighborhood. Tiger turns his shoulders nearly 120 degrees and has his left shoulder some 18-20 inches behind the ball. Incredible! Being young and talented certainly helps him out a great deal. Most of us will never achieve this much turn but can use Tiger as the ultimate. The further you turn your shoulders, the further you'll hit the ball. Period.

What most golfers do is this. Instead of turning back with the shoulders and triangle, most average players swing the club back with their arms. Their club goes back, their arms go back, but their body doesn't. Rather than getting their body to turn back, only their arms take the club back. This is, and will always be, a weak move. That big, strong body, which supplies so much of the power, hasn't done a thing, and only the light, little arms and club have become involved. Ten pounds of arms are not going to hit the ball as far as 170 pounds of body. This player has the sensation of lifting the club up in the air instead of turning the body back. His right shoulder may turn slightly, (30-45 degrees) but that's not going to get the job done. The right shoulder doesn't turn back

Photo 23:No shoulder turn.

behind the ball either. It stays in a position that is still in front of the golf ball. That would be like trying to shoot your slingshot without first pulling the rubber band back. It's not going to do anything! *Photo 23* shows the difference.

In *Photo 20, I've* kept my triangle

together and have turned my right shoulder behind the ball. Even though the club and arms are waist high, my body has turned considerably. The player in *Photo 23* has lifted her club up quite high but has not turned her body very much. This player has created a feeling of taking a big backswing, but is only fooling herself. The club may be back quite far, but the shoulders have not done their job.

Keep your triangle. As your shoulders turn back behind the ball in your 90-degree shoulder turn, a bit more of your weight goes back to the left leg. You don't thrust it over there on purpose. It just moves there naturally as your body turns. You have just, "pulled the rubber band back." From this position your body can eventually transfer its weight back through the ball over to your right leg. This weight transfer happens on the downswing and adds power and distance to your golf shots.

The player that swings only the club and arms up, without turning his shoulders, loses this powerful shifting movement. Most of his weight stays on his right foot during the backswing because his shoulders don't turn back. If you just stand still and lift your arms up in the air, nothing happens to your weight. Keeping your weight on the right foot eliminates any chance of driving powerfully though the ball because you never went back to begin with. You can't shift over to your right leg because you're already there. You didn't pull back your rubber band. This lack of weight transfer is usually referred to as a "reverse weight shift." Your weight is shifting opposite of where you want your ball to go. Instead of moving over to your right

leg on the downswing and ending up on your left toe, you do the opposite and fall over backwards. Without the proper movements on your backswing, your downswing will never be very effective.

If we go back to the address position for a moment, we now realize how important that tilt was for turning your triangle back correctly. If your tilt isn't there, your head will be too far in front of the ball at address, and getting a 90-degree shoulder turn is impossible. Your weight will not transfer back and through, and nothing very good is ever going to happen. Just remember that your stance has to be correct if your fundamentals have any chance of succeeding. With you head tilted back, as it should be, you can turn your shoulders back where they should be.

Seeing the Triangle and Shoulder Turn in Other Sports

This triangle is not unique to a golf swing. Many sports and everyday motions move in a similar way. Looking at a few of them may give you a clearer picture and feeling of what the triangle should feel like.

When a tennis pro swings back to hit a forehand shot (a left-handed player) the right shoulder turns behind the ball as the shoulders turn 90 degrees. The weight has moved to the left leg. The "V" of their shirt looks back at the head of the racket. From this position, the pro can drive through the ball with the legs shifting weight over to the right leg.

When an outfielder rears back to throw a baseball into home plate, his weight shifts as the shoulders turn back. The further back he reaches, the further he'll throw the ball. Even a discus thrower turns his body back before hurling the discus forward. Virtually every sport where the goal is to move an object from one location to another contains these movements. The shoulders and upper body turn back, with the weight transferring to the left leg before uncoiling powerfully toward the target. All the weight moves forward onto the right leg. The object (football, tennis racquet, baseball bat, golf club) is pulled through last.

The Handshake

At this time I want to add a new word to your golfing vocabulary. The previous pages have been talking

Photo 24: At address.

about the triangle and shoulder turn. But now it's time to make your job even easier. Instead of continuing to say and think "triangle," we're now going to say "handshake" or "shake hands."

Most of us don't use the word tri-

angle on a daily basis; it simply doesn't come up in conversation very much. Something we all do everyday is shake someone's hand. The simple act of turning to shake hands with someone is now going to be your thought as you stand at your address position. *Photo 24* shows the golfer at the address position. Without holding a club, turn your right hand back like you're starting your swing and shake hands with someone. This person is standing directly behind you on the target line. When you shake hands, your right arm and hand will be waist high. They are in the same position as the triangle was. As *Photo 25* shows,

Photo 25: "The Handshake."

your right shoulder has turned behind the golf ball and your shoulders have turned 90 degrees. How easy is that! All the elements that were crucial in the triangle exercise are now there when you shake hands. Your left hand follows along with the right, creating the triangle position and the "V" of your shirt is looking directly at the other person.

Your weight has transferred back to your left leg and your body is coiled quite fully. From this position the body is now ready to explode through the ball, pulling the club down and through the ball. The left hand comes through the impact position and "shakes hands" on the other side of the ball. When this happens, the body moves up onto the left toe and the triangle is intact, waist high, on the follow through. You'll be up on your left toe with almost all of your weight now

Photo 26: Weight is now on your right leg.

on your right leg. (See *Photo 26*.) Your handshake on the backswing turns your body and shoulders correctly, loading up your left side, and your handshake on the downswing transfers your weight over to your right side, turning your shoulders forward. You've pulled the rubber band on your slingshot back and fired it through, toward your target.

When I am teaching students the handshake move, I turn their triangle back to waist high and show them how their right shoulder has turned a few inches behind the ball. I have them hit their 7 iron with this half-swing feeling. I turn them back to just waist high on their backswing, and then have them shake hands on their downswing. Don't feel like you have to cut off your follow through at waist high. It's next to impossible and you shouldn't even try. Go ahead and let the club swing all the way up to your finish. What is helpful though, is to only go back half way for a while. Your 7 iron should go about 100 yards.

Many of you may be surprised how far your ball flies with this half swing. Some students actually hit the ball farther with the handshake swing than they did with their old "full swing." This is the key ingredient of the handshake. Even though your club and arms swing only half way back, your shoulders are turning further, sometimes even double or triple the amount they were turning with your old swing. Your body is turning more than it used to, which will of course lead to increased power. Rather than just swinging back with a little bit of weight, you're now turning back with most of your body weight. Not only are you turning your body and shoulders, but you are also shifting all of this weight back and forth. The tennis player's weight goes back before it comes forward, like an outfielder throwing a baseball. If either of these athletes only moved his arms back he would never get enough power to move the ball or racquet very fast.

At this point, don't worry about taking the club back too far. Just work on the half swing and half-speed handshake for a while. Don't worry what your club should do as it goes farther back, or worry about the top of your swing. These elements will all fall into place and will happen quite naturally. You want to hit hundreds of these little shots before trying to hit the big ones.

The Accuracy of the Handshake

The last part of your handshake will have a significant influence on how straight you hit your shots. Everything you have learned about the handshake so far has dealt with increasing your power. But power without accuracy is a waste of time.

When your club is waist high in the handshake position, the shaft should be parallel to your toes. The club you're holding is also parallel to the club that's lying on the ground, pointing at your target. You have just pulled your rubber band straight back. If your club goes back straight, it's going to come down straight. With your club in its correct position, at waist high, I want you to notice something. The hole in the end of your grip, (take a look, it's there) is pointing directly at your target. If there was a laser beam shining out of this hole it would shine right at your target.

Most golfers swing their club around their body like a baseball bat. In the waist high position, if your club goes around you, the grip or laser beam will be pointing into the left woods. This is a very common problem with students because many of them are actually trying to get their club around their bodies. Somewhere, someone told them to swing their club "inside-out." They've been told that this inside move on their backswing cures their slice and you see them wrapping their club back like a tennis racquet.

No, no, no! In most cases, I would say this is what causes their slice. With the club so far behind them and their grip pointing way to the left, their club comes down and hits the ball to the left. The club goes back inside the target line and naturally swings out to left

Photo 27: Starting to go inside.

Photo 28: Way inside the target line. Like a baseball bat.

field too much on the downswing. If you held your slingshot and pulled the rubber band back sideways like this, it would shoot out sideways as it snapped through. Photos 27 and 28 show the difference. I think it is indisputable.

Here is another reason the ball may slice. With the club so far behind you, your arms feel like they have no room to swing down on the forward swing. Your legs are in the way. Since the arms can't drop in where they should, they lift up and around your body, and approach the ball from outside the target line. The club cuts across the ball and a slice is all but guaranteed. The very move they were trying to prevent (the "over the top" slice) is all but guaranteed. With the club in the correct handshake position, it can come down into the ball on the correct line.

Photo 29: Swinging inside.

Photo 29 shows you what "inside" actually looks like. It is important that you have a complete understanding of what should be happening.

The club lying on the ground is your target line. It's the line the ball flies on. Anything left of the line is what we will call outside. Anything right of the line is inside. Photo 29 shows the player in the handshake position with the shaft pointing directly at the target. The club is parallel to the target line, but is some 18-20 inches inside the line. This is what inside means. The club is closer to you than

the target line, but is in a parallel position. *Photo 30* shows the wrong way to swing inside. This player has

Photo 30: Swinging too far inside.

wrapped the club around his body too much and the shaft of his club is no longer parallel to the target line. The laser beam out of the grip is shining way off to the left and the player is going to have a difficult time squaring

Photo 31A: Coming down "outside.".

up the clubface.

Photo 31A shows how the player must lift the arms and club up and out to have enough room for the club to swing down into the ball. The club has looped way up and around and now approaches the ball from outside the ideal line. Swinging down from outside to inside creates the big slice that so many of us have. Any picture of a Tour pro in a golf magazine usually has the pro in this 'handshake' position. From Byron Nelson and Jack Nicklaus, to Davis Love and Tiger Woods, all great players have the club parallel to their toes at waist high on their back swings. So should you.

Another valuable checkpoint in your handshake is the label, or emblem, on your golf glove. When you're in your handshake position, make sure this label is facing out, not up. If you actually turned back to shake hands with someone, the back of your right hand faces out, not skyward. Rolling the right hand skyward opens your clubface on the backswing, and makes it that much harder to square it up when you swing down. You wouldn't shake hands with someone with your palm facing the ground would you? In *Photo 31B.* you can clearly see the back of my hand facing

Photo 31B: Back of hand faces out.

outward.

On your forward swing, make sure your left hand "handshake" also has the correct movement. The back of your left hand should face out when

it's at waist high on the follow through. Many golfers have their left palm facing skyward at this point, which leaves the clubface wide open. The left hand rolls during the start of your follow through and the left palm eventually faces the ground as you near shoulder height. I don't like telling a student to "roll your wrists" during his swing, but the wrist roll does happen. It should be a natural movement in a correct swing. Keeping the wrists from rolling, or flipping them through excessively, can only lead to poor ball striking. Your hands and arms follow the lead of the shoulders and body.

Your first week of learning the handshake should consist of the following.

A)   Lay your two clubs on the ground for your alignment and ball position.

B)   Take your address position and use your 7 iron.

C)   Tee all your shots.

D)   Turn your triangle back to waist high. Make sure the shaft is parallel to your toes and your right shoulder is turning behind the ball. Your arms will go to just past your waist with little or no wrist cocking.

E)   Come down and hit the tee. Keying on the tee instead of the ball reduces your desire to swing too hard.

F)   Turn the triangle through to waist high and continue up into your finish position.

G)   Your body should face the target and you should be up on your left toe.

Starting your backswing correctly lets you finish your backswing correctly, and allows you to strike the ball with power and accuracy on your downswing. The way you actually strike the golf ball and arrive at your follow through is dictated by this first move back away from the ball during the backswing. Different ideas work for different people. It makes no difference if you think, "handshake," "triangle," or turn the right shoulder behind the ball, you are doing the same thing. The idea of "turning your back to the target," or "hitting your chin with your right shoulder" are also effective ways to help you turn away from the ball, and all achieve that all-important move of getting your body involved in your backswing.

You must first learn the half swing before trying to master the full swing. Through a few buckets of balls, you will gradually get longer and longer as you swing back, but this extra part of the swing is not as important as the handshake. Where the handshake was clearly visible in all the good swings I analyzed, the top of the swing was different on many of them. Almost every Tour pro had his club in the handshake position, but I must have seen 30 different positions when these pros arrived at the top of their swings. The way you arrive at the top has a great deal to do with your height, arm length, and body type, and is the one element of the golf swing that is different for most golfers. We'll get into this a bit later. For now; don't worry about where you are at the top, practice the handshake and half swing.

Chapter Four:
Fundamental 2: "The Wall"

Chapter Four: Fundamental 2: The Wall

Your second fundamental is also part of your backswing. Chapter Three dealt with how your upper body, arms and club swing back during your "handshake," but there is another part of your body that has an important job to do: your lower body. Fundamental Two is about "what your legs should do on the backswing." As you turn back and shake hands, what is happening to your legs?

From my experience, this is the most overlooked and under taught part of the golf swing. Most books talk about your grip and shoulder turn, and how your body moves into the ball on the downswing. But very few of them cover what your legs do on the *backswing*, and it's definitely important. If your legs don't do what they're supposed to on the *backswing*, they will never be able to do their job properly on the *downswing*.

Your legs should remain very firm and stable during the backswing, much like the walls of your house do. There are several parts of the wall, and discussing them one at a time will give you clear goals when you practice them on the range.

Analyzing the Wall

The first part of "the wall" is your left leg. The left leg serves as an anchor during the backswing, much like the walls of your home serve as the foundation. As your upper body turns back during your handshake, the left leg should stay almost as solid as a wall. It will have some slight hinging and flexing, and should never feel rigid, but should stay quite steady. The upper body is doing its best to turn the

shoulders back behind the ball, but the left leg is trying equally as hard to remain firm. Ben Hogan used to lean a golf club against his leg and try not to knock it over as he swung back. Your

Photo 32: Maintaining The Wall.".

right shoulder is turning and your left leg is doing nothing. See *Photo 32*.

Every athlete in every sport has a wall. As a left-handed tennis pro swings back, he plants his left leg and swings around it. His upper body turns way back, but his legs stay put. A baseball player does the same thing. He rears back to throw the ball but doesn't move the back leg.

Your weight shifts over to the left leg, but never goes outside, beyond that wall. Keep your weight on your instep. I tell my students, "Swing into your left leg, not outside of it." This wall also keeps you more centered over the ball, which makes it easier to return squarely, back to where you started when you swing down. Look for the wall next time you watch a professional golfer on TV.

On their backswing, what many amateurs do is get outside their left leg and knock the wall over. As their shoulders turn back, their whole body sways back. Instead of keeping a solid

Photo 33A: Knocking "The Wall" over.

foundation with their legs, they almost fall over backwards as they turn their upper body. *Photo 33A* shows a golfer knocking the wall over on the backswing. Her weight is on the outside of her left foot, her knee is jutting out, and her legs have collapsed. If your legs are "in the next county," it's going to be next to impossible to find your way back to the ball.

Imagine a tennis pro swinging back and looking like this. He would never be able to drive forward and hit the ball with any effectiveness from this position. The outfielder would throw the ball about 2 feet if he knocked his wall over. Most golfers I see get so caught up in what their club is doing on the backswing, they never pay attention to their wall. Your legs are

the only things that touch the ground. Their role is crucial. Simply keep your left leg in the same position it was in during your address. What you're doing, in reality, is nothing. You're just keeping your left leg the same as you turn your shoulders and upper body fully behind the ball.

The Right Leg

Your right leg should also remain quite still. Keep your right heel on the ground. When you swing back, try to keep your right heel planted. If your right heel or leg moves too much you'll probably knock your wall over. Venturi stated, "If you're physically able, I recommend keeping your left (in our case, right) heel on the ground." Fifty years ago Ben Hogan wrote, "The left heel (in our case, right again) should stay on the ground. It may move an inch, but no more." If your right heel moves too much you're only asking for trouble.

Six Reasons Why Picking Up the Right Heel is Bad

1. If you pick the right heel up, you'll knock the left leg wall over.

2. If the right heel comes up, you're not back toward your heels anymore.

3. If the right heel comes up, you'll stand up and may hit the ball thin.

4. If the right heel comes up, you have to put it back. That's more stuff you have to do.

5. If the right heel comes up, you may put it back in the wrong place, which may cause everything to be in the wrong place.

6. You can't start down correctly if you are up on your right toe.

Notice that Venturi said, "If you're physically able." If your flexibility is

40

Photo 33B: Not keeping the right heel down causes many problems.

not very good or you have a bad back, you may need to lift the heel a little to get enough shoulder turn. But most of us should keep the heel down. A heavy person or a senior player may also have a reduction in their flexibility, but in my teaching career I have had only a handful of students who needed to lift the right heel. *(Photo 33B.)*

Bobby Jones, Arnold Palmer, and Jack Nicklaus all picked up their front heel a little, but that's the way golf used to be taught in their era. Since then, not only have teachers gotten better educated, but equipment has changed and the golf swing has evolved along with these factors. Golfers of the past also hit range balls every day and were talented enough to put the heel back. Nicklaus started his downswing by slamming his heel back onto the ground. He picked up it, so he had to put it back. Jack could also raise his left heel without knocking over the right leg wall, but most students I see sway backwards when the heel rises. Keeping your right heel down falls into the category of asking you to do nothing. Just don't move it.

As an instructor, sometimes the hardest thing for me to get students to do is to do less. Trying to get them to stop doing something is every bit as hard as getting them to do something more. They're so used to raising the right heel, it seems like it takes forever to stop. With some time on the range, however, golfers begin to understand that doing less is much easier.

Keep the Flex

When I'm showing a student the wall, the third element I address is knee flex. The left leg stays solid, the right heel stays down, but you must make sure both knees stay flexed. Your legs are flexed at address and they should stay flexed throughout your backswing.

Our tennis pro and outfielder certainly maintain the flex in their legs when they turn back. So should you. In fact, many of the Tour professionals actually flex their back knee more as they reach the top of the swing. They turn their club and upper body back and squat down into their back knee. Nicklaus did this move quite clearly. At his address, Nicklaus' knees were slightly flexed, and at the top of his swing they were noticeably flexed more. Like a tennis pro, who goes down on his backswing, Nicklaus swung into the flex of his back knee, then sprung up off it during the downswing. This extra squat is a move that I would reserve thinking about until you are a low handicapper. Just make sure you keep your knees flexed the same as they were at address.

Most golfers tend to straighten their left leg on the backswing. As they turn back with the upper body and club, they stand up. Instead of maintaining the flex in their left leg, it's

Photo 34: A stiff left leg is useless in the backswing

now stiff as a board and is, quite frankly, useless. See *Photo 34*.

What happens when you lose your flex?

Far and away, the most common bad shot that results when you stand up is hitting a thin or topped shot. It's really very easy to understand. During your backswing, if your left leg straightens up, your whole body raises. Instead of being at the same height relative to the ball, you're now higher than where you started. You go up, so your club goes up. You either top it, hit it thin, or worse, whiff it entirely. Usually your friend will say, "Hey Joe, you picked your head up." You then reply, "I could have sworn I kept it down." You're not picking your head up when you top it, you're **standing up**. Because you lost the flex in your knees, your body isn't in the same height relative to the ground as it was in during your address position. The legs straighten, so the body straightens

and this is what you perceive as your head going up.

You may hit a pull or a push as well. When your left leg straightens, it's dead. You just can't move a stiff or straight leg. Since your legs are useless at this point, only your arms swing down, bringing the club with them. The pull happens because your arms pass your legs too soon (since your legs didn't move) and the ball goes off to the right. If your legs had been flexed, they would have been able to drive through the ball better on the downswing and pulled the arms down correctly. The left leg just stood there and the upper body and arms did all the work coming down.

The last ugly shot that may result is the direct opposite, a push or slice off to the left. Since the left leg is stiff and useless, it cannot help out on the downswing. Your lower body can't turn through fully on your downswing, so your arms and club don't square up. You hit off to the left. Some people would say, "You didn't roll your wrists." Well almost, but not exactly. Your arms didn't turn over as they should have, because your body didn't drive through as it should have. This happened because you straightened your left leg and it couldn't help on the downswing. There was little, if any, drive with your legs. The inadequate leg drive prevented your entire lower body from turning through the ball. This made your arms swing out toward left field without having any chance at all to roll over and square up the clubface. That label on your glove was in the wrong position, which kept the clubface open, and you sliced or pushed your shot.

You've got a 50-50 chance of

either pushing or pulling your ball when you straighten your left leg. Sometimes your arms turn over and pass your body (the pull). At other times the arms drift out to the left (the push). In any case, keep your knees flexed during the backswing on every club, from your driver down to your wedges.

The easiest way I can explain how your legs spring through the ball is this. If you try to jump up in the air off of stiff or straight legs, you can't even move. To jump up, your legs have to be flexed. You must lower yourself down, bending your knees, before your spring up into the air, right?

You can also think about the zipper on your trousers. At address, the zipper on your pants is looking at the golf

turn. You should almost be able to get your arms and club waist high without moving your zipper. The wire still looks down where it was at address. Keeping your wire still will ensure that you're not swaying back with your lower body. Your left knee wall is solid, your right heel has stayed down, and you've kept your flex. The image of the wire does it all for you.

Once your arms and club have reached the handshake position, you physically can't turn any further unless your zipper turns back a little. But this movement is minimal. Ben Hogan said that the zipper on your pants should never turn past your back toe. Even with your driver, when you're at the top of your swing, your zipper should only point at your left toe,

Photo 35: "The Wire."

Photo 36: Zipper points at the left toe.

ball. Now imagine a wire attached to your zipper and anchored at the golf tee, as in *Photo 35*. When you start your backswing with your handshake going back, your shoulders start to

never beyond it. Take a look at *Photo 36* to see what I mean.

Tiger Woods, Fred Couples and David Duval are the best players to watch to see the wire staying still. At the top of their backswings, their zippers have moved only an inch or two back from where they started. By restricting the movement of their lower bodies and turning their shoulders more than 90 degrees, they have created an enormous amount of torque in their golf swings, which is where they get their massive power.

When I'm teaching my own students, I explain it to them this way. Imagine you're holding a spring or a slinky. Hold the bottom of it tight and don't move it. Now grab the top of it and twist it. You're coiling the upper part around the lower part. You get to a point where you can't hold it anymore because of the torsion. From this point, if you let go of the top it pops back into place with great speed. The simple act of winding the upper part around the lower part made it unwind when you let go of it.

This is what your body should do in the golf swing. Your legs (the bottom of the spring, the wall) stay quite still on the backswing, while your upper body and shoulders turn around them. The more you turn your shoulders back, while keeping your lower body still, the more you create the torsion you need to hit the ball far. Woods, Couples and Duval do this as well as anyone on the Tour. They turn their shoulders more than 100 degrees, while keeping their legs very still. The coil they create is truly amazing and is the dominant reason they're able to routinely hit drives over 300 yards. While most of us can't get that much coil, we can work on creating as much as possible by keeping our own legs solid on the backswing.

When you sway back and knock your wall over, you lose any chance of getting this coil. If your zipper or wire move too much on the backswing, it's impossible to wind up enough to get any power in your down swing. When your zipper moves out past your left toe, your lower body has turned back too much. What you will find is that your shoulders and legs have both moved back nearly the same distance, eliminating your coil. Think about it for a second. If your upper body turns back 90 degrees, and your lower body also moves back 90 degrees you're not winding anything around anything else.

Your first week of learning the Wall should consist of the following.

A).Take your address position and notice how your legs look.

B) Swing back about ten inches and try to keep your zipper in line with the ball.

C) Get to the handshake position and stop.

D) Make sure your left leg stays quiet, without swaying laterally back. Your weight should be on your left instep.

E) See if your right heel is still down.

F) Make sure your knees are still flexed.

G) Your zipper should point at your left toe and no further.

H) Continue your swing back without moving your lower body any further.

Keeping your lower body quiet just makes sense. If you don't move the lower body too much on the backswing, you'll be able to find the ball much more often when you swing down. You've eliminated wasted movement and have a swing that is easier for you to repeat. Your swing will feel a bit tighter or more compact, and the creation of coil will be quite noticeable. You'll feel the stretch in the right side of your torso as you swing back and may notice that your swing is not as long as it was before. Even though your club is going back a bit less, you'll hit the ball farther! You have increased the torsion in your swing. You'll unwind through the ball with great power now, and find that your follow through is looking pretty good as well.

One last bit of the wall that applies to many golfers has to do with over-swinging. Countless golfers swing the club way too far back on their back-swings. Their club and arms go way beyond parallel when they reach the top. It looks like they've almost hit their ankles. Having any control is impossible and hitting the ball the same way twice is going to be very difficult. The reason many golfers get in this position is because they knock their wall over. When their legs give way, their arms and club flop at the top. If their walls had remained solid and their whole lower body motion was reduced, they physically couldn't go back so far. The solid lower body would make them more solid at the top.

To see this for yourself, try hitting a ball off your knees. What you'll quickly discover is that you can't over-swing at the top. When the average player tightens up his lower body, he shortens his swing at the top. The next time you play with someone that has a severe over-swing, look at his legs. Both of them will be swaying back too much and he'll probably be lifting his right heel off the ground. Your down-swing will be much more consistent and effective if your backswing is more solid. Speaking of the down-swing, let's go on to *Fundamental Three*.

Chapter Five:
Fundamental 3:"The Zipper"

Chapter Five: Fundamental 3: The Zipper

Up to this point, you have learned how to properly address the golf ball and start your backswing. The handshake and wall have guided you through your job on the takeaway and have given you ways to check that you're in the proper position. If you have gone to the range already and tried the first two fundamentals, you're properly hitting the ball quite well. As the previous chapter discussed, a shot of a hundred yards is what you should be trying to achieve. But you shouldn't be surprised if you're hitting it farther than your full shots used to go, using your old swing. The simple act of turning your upper body around your wall on your backswing creates enough torsion to hit the ball surprisingly far distances.

I often joke with my students at the start of our third lesson by saying, "You're hitting the ball better and farther than you used to, and I still haven't told you how to come down yet."

Yet they are hitting the ball better because they're swinging back better. If you swing back correctly, you're going to swing down correctly. Our slingshot analogy has shown us this several times. After you have mastered your first two fundamentals, and have become comfortable performing them, it's time to learn how to swing down. Even though you may already be swinging down better than you used to, it is helpful to have a clear plan for starting your downswing. This is what fundamental # 3 will show you.

Breaking down Fundamental # 3

When a golfer reaches the top of his backswing, what's next? What moves first? What should you be feeling? The answer to all these questions is the legs. From the top of your swing, your lower body will start the downswing initiating the forward movement. The legs start shifting your weight from your left leg to your right, with the rest of your body following along. Finally your arms and club are pulled powerfully into the ball propelling it down the fairway. Sounds simple.

Think of an outfielder rearing back to throw a baseball into the infield again. The first part of his body that moves forward is his legs. He steps forward and throws. Where his weight was totally on his left leg when he reared back, it's now moving over to his right as he steps. The last thing that comes forward is his arm. A batter at home plate "steps into the pitch" to hit the ball. He was coiled back as the pitcher started to throw, and then moved his right leg forward. His bat explodes through the ball as his arms are pulled through. Even a bowler walks toward the line with his legs leading the swinging of his arms. Because the ball is heavy, the bowler needed the weight and strength of his body to propel his arms through toward the pins.

In every one of these movements the legs initiated the down stroke. The object these players were holding came down last. A golf swing is exactly the same. The legs and lower body drive forward first, pulling the arms and club down last. The arms are simply not big, strong or heavy enough to create enough power on their own. They need some help. To immediately impress upon you how important the legs are, imagine hitting a golf ball while sitting on a chair. Without your lower body you could only hit the ball a few yards. Mark McGuire could never hit the ball out of the park if he just swung his arms. You'll never drive the ball anywhere if you don't get your legs involved.

The movement of starting your lower body first has been described in a hundred different ways. It doesn't matter what you think of, as long as your legs go first.

Ben Hogan used to turn his hips toward the target. Arnold Palmer would get his knees moving forward. Nicklaus put his front heel down. Everyone has his or her personal favorite. Here's the one I teach my students that has always been easy for them to learn.

At the top of your backswing, your zipper is pointing at your left toe. Remember? To start down, turn your zipper to the target. The first thing you do is turn the zipper so it faces the target. It's like a string is attached to your zipper and this string pulls your zipper around so it faces the target. Your zipper passes the ball well before your arms and club come down. At impact, your zipper has turned forward so far that it's a good foot or two in front of the ball. Most of your weight is on your right foot, and your left heel is coming off the ground. Your left knee is moving in toward your right and the gap between your knees is now only a few inches, as in *Photo 37A*. Your club is still a few feet away from the ball at this point, and 90% of the weight is on

the right leg. The left leg is firing in and the left heel is a few inches off the ground.

Clearly, the arms and club are being pulled down and through the golf ball. The arms follow along for the ride, squaring up the clubface at impact. The hands and arms have done the necessary rolling, and have done so naturally at quite a high rate of speed.

The hips turn, the knees move, and the entire lower body is participating in the swing. Every single ounce of your weight is now helping to add power and distance to your shot.

Long hitters like Tiger Woods and John Daly, turn through faster and more aggressively than most other professionals, with their zipper almost facing the target at impact. Their back heel is off the ground more than the

Photo 37A: Your left knee is moving in toward your right and the gap between your knees is now only a few inches.

others and their knees are almost touching. The faster your legs move, the farther you'll hit the ball.

Your zipper (you could also think your belly button) is your center of gravity. It's the middle of your body. It's a very clear, easy to key on element in your swing. When you turn it toward the target, everything else will come down right where you want them.

Without the correct lower body move, you are only hitting the ball with your arms. If your legs don't turn through the shot, only your arms and club come down. This always results in a poor, powerless shot. As in the stance, handshake, and wall, there are several bad shots that result if you don't start the zipper first: weak shot, fat shot, pull, push and top.

The weak shot doesn't go anywhere. If the lower body doesn't drive powerfully through the ball, only the arms hit it. Remember, the arms just aren't big and strong enough to let you hit the ball very far. When the legs stand still and the arms do all the work, it's called "over the top." The arms come over and around the legs (since the legs don't get out of the way) and you end up a weak, off-line shot.

The fat shot happens because your weight stayed over your left foot too much. The club hits the ground at the low spot and you hit several inches behind the ball. With the zipper going first, you get your weight over to your right leg, which lets you hit the ball before the ground.

The pull comes from your arms and club passing you, (since your legs didn't move) and swinging around you, to the right. The club flipped through rolling your wrists, closing the clubface excessively. Try standing with your feet together. Now, holding the club, swing back and forth. You'll feel your arms really wrap around you

on the follow through and realize that your hands are doing too much. Your legs couldn't move in this exercise because your feet were together, making them useless.

Although a push is the exact opposite of a pull, it too is also the result of not driving the lower body through. If your zipper doesn't turn when you're impacting the ball, your zipper is pointing out to left field. The lower body didn't turn at all, so the club doesn't turn either. In other words, if your zipper is slow going through the ball, your clubface will be slow squaring up. The result of course, is an open clubface, which causes the push or slice.

Finally, we get the thin shot. When the legs don't turn through, they tend to straighten up slightly to maintain your body's balance. Instead of driving down and through, they lazily stand in the way and your arms don't reach down as far as they normally would. Because the arms are a bit higher than they should be, you hit the ball thin, above its equator. If it's not a grounder, it's rather thin and doesn't go as far as it should.

Get those legs involved in your swing. It is crucial to success.

How the Wall and Zipper Are Connected.

Any of the five bad shots just discussed may happen if your lower body and zipper don't do their job on the downswing. A poor leg drive is one of the most common problems I deal with on a daily basis with my own students.

The most common reason for a poor zipper turn is because you knock your wall over on the backswing.

Without a solid wall to keep you in place on your backswing, you'll never be able to start down with the zipper. If you sway or fall over backwards on your backswing, your legs can't possibly drive forward on your downswing. They just can't. Having your weight too much outside your wall when you're at the top of your swing prevents you from shifting it over to your right leg as you swing down. Your wall is tremendously important to your zipper. In the last chapter, I mentioned how Jack Nicklaus has a springy feeling in his back leg at the top of his backswing when he "keeps his flex." Because his knee is so lively, he can drive off his back leg with great power. He can turn his zipper through the ball because his wall and flex were so good on his backswing.

Photo 37B: Motion of the left knee.

As I mentioned, the other common problem I see often is raising the right heel. If your right heel raises up too much on your backswing, it will be very difficult to start your legs down first. It's nearly impossible to get your weight over to your right leg if you're up on your right toe. Make sure your wall is solid before you start working on your zipper.

Other ways to do the zipper could include, "getting your knees together," "hitting the ball with your left knee," or "getting your left knee to the ball before the club gets to the ball." All these are simply options for you to try out. See which one works best for you.

Photo 37B shows the left knee idea. The player has pushed off his left foot and his knee is even with the ball long before the club ever gets there.

At the top of your follow through, your weight is 95% on your right leg, your knees are together, you're up on

Photo 38:The ideal follow through.

your left toe, and your zipper is facing the target. In *Photo 38* I am in what I consider the ideal follow through position. The golfer in *Photo 39* however, has not turned his lower body forward and still has the majority of his weight on his left leg. This doesn't even look right. Imagine throwing a baseball and ending up in this position. Just about every athlete imaginable ends up on the back toe, with all the weight over on the front leg. It works better, it is

*Photo 39: Too much weight
on left leg.*

better, and it even looks better.

The Best Move in Golf

Whatever you need to think about, feel, or do, to get your lower body starting down first should be your goal for your downswing. We have seen that ten different golfers may think of ten different ideas, but the result is the same: The lower body is turning toward the target. What works well for one student, may not work for another. It's up to you to try a few of them out and discover which works best.

Under this premise, I'm now going to give you another way to initiate your downswing, which I think is "the best move in golf." Strong words to be sure, but in my own students' cases, this is the one move they all seem to do the best, achieve the best results with, and learn the quickest. It may well be the most used move on the tour as well, with more than half the professionals that I spoke with using it. They're all still starting with the lower body, but their thought is on something different.

Believe it or not, the new move or thought that I want you to try is with your upper body. Are you still standing? That's right, the best move in golf involves thinking about your upper body. Most of my students say, "What? You just spent a whole lesson teaching me to start my legs and zipper down first, now you're telling me to start down with my upper body?" Not exactly. I'm going to have you think about an upper body part. This thought is simply going to get your lower body even more active on your downswing.

The upper body part is your right shoulder. Back at our handshake lesson, you wanted to turn your right shoulder back behind the ball. A good three or four inches was your goal. Well, as long as you're thinking about your right shoulder, we're going to keep on thinking about it as we *pull it out of the way as soon as possible.* You were very conscious about getting it behind the ball on the backswing, now pull it out of the way. When you do this through to completion, you'll notice that your legs and zipper have done their job in a beautiful fashion. When your shoulder turns through, so does everything else. At the top of your follow through, your chest is facing the target (it may even be slightly right of the target), your zipper is pointing straight, your knees are together, and you're up on your left toe. The upper body turned and naturally pulled the rest of the body with it.

What's so interesting is when I videotaped all my students doing this move, then played the tape back in ultra-slow motion, it was actually the legs that moved first. The students' whole thought was on the right shoulder pulling, and it did. But doing this actually made the lower body start first!

I tell my students, "You're not hitting these balls better because your shoulder is pulling, you're hitting them better because when your right shoulder pulls, it is making your legs go better." You simply have to end up in the correct position when you pull your shoulder through. Your body will be in a straight-line position, which puts no strain on your lower back.

The only flaw in the zipper idea is something I see in about 10% of my students. They understand what the zipper should do but still can't turn it through enough. They end up with a bit too much weight still on their left

Photo 40: The "Reverse C."

foot and have their upper body arching back a bit., as in *Photo 40*. Their zipper turned some but still points into left field slightly. This position is called a "Reverse C" and was actually taught in the 1970's. Most of us today however, feel it ruined more golf swings (and lower backs) than it helped. You feel like you're sort of hanging back when you do this. By pulling the right shoulder, you all but

eliminate this Reverse C. Even Bryon Nelson and Ben Hogan ended up in a more vertical position with their shoulders and knees more lined up with each other. Great examples of this good follow through position on today's Tour include Tiger Woods, Davis Love, Justin Leonard and Steve Elkington.

For you experienced golfers, I know what you may be thinking. "If I pull my right shoulder out of the way too fast I'm going to hit a 90 yard hook." Allow me to explain how just the opposite will happen. Remember the expression, "coming over the top." Coming over the top is when your upper body starts the downswing before the legs start turning through. The left shoulder thrusts the arms and club out and around the legs, "coming over the top" of the swing. This usually results in a badly pulled shot to the right, or if the clubface is open, a pull-slice. Golfers with little or no leg drive (zipper turn) come over the top on almost every shot they hit. Their left shoulder gets outside their right during the downswing.

Well, if you pull your right shoulder out of the way, your left shoulder can't come over the right shoulder if it's not there! There is no way the left shoulder can overtake the right shoulder if it's pulling forward and turning through the shot. When the right shoulder pulls powerfully from the top (remember it's actually your legs that are moving first), the rest of your body will follow along, bringing your arms, hands, and club squarely into the golf ball. Your zipper will turn completely through and will pull you up onto your left toe.

If your shoulder pull (leg drive) is

fast and powerful, you're body will move through ahead of the ball, well before your club gets there. If it's too far ahead you'll actually push or block the ball. Where you may have thought this move would cause a pull, it may actually promote a push to the left. There is no way the club will flip through and pass your body too early if your body is out in front.

To get the feeling of the right shoulder pulling, try this drill. Take your address position and grip the club by the head end, with only your right arm. Take your normal backswing and stop at the top. From here, pull your right shoulder through. With the club being upside down, and the right arm holding on, you'll really get the feeling of whipping through the shot. Without the left arm hanging on, the energy of the pull will almost "screw you" into the ground, and make your entire body move through to your right leg. Although your legs are actually moving better and faster, it feels like your upper body is doing all the work. A note of caution here. Do not try this one armed drill holding your club by the grip end as you normally would. The weight of the clubhead will jerk your right shoulder badly if you're not careful. The pulling of the right shoulder motion is a great way to get your lower body involved in the downswing. Most of my own students like this idea more than any other, and it has improved their ball striking dramatically.

Your Head

One detail you also want to check is that your head stays behind the ball as your club strikes it. At address, your right ear was lined up over the ball and

your head was behind it. At the top of your swing, your head naturally moves back slightly as you turn your shoulders, and ends up nearly over your left knee. Some golfers try furiously to not move their head at all, but this is not right. There is no way to turn your body and shoulders behind the ball if your head doesn't "go with the flow."

Trying to keep the head absolutely still prohibits the shoulders from getting any turn and creates a reverse weight shift. That is, your weight moves to your right leg instead of your left. With all the weight on the right leg, the only place it can move to is your left leg. Your weight is shifting in the wrong direction as you swing down. Creating any power is next to impossible. Having your "tilt" at address pre-sets your head behind the ball slightly, and lets the upper body have a better and fuller turn on the backswing.

With your shoulders at their full 90-degree turn, and your head near your left knee, you now begin your downswing. Your weight starts moving over to your right leg, as your hips, zipper and lower body unwind through the downswing. Make sure that as this downswing action happens, you keep your head back, behind the ball. Your weight shifts, your zipper turns, and your legs drive, but your head must stay back behind the ball. In order for your arms to square the clubface up, they must pass you at some point, so you can hit the ball straight. Keeping your head back allows this to happen, and happen quite naturally. If your head moves forward, toward the target, your arms cannot pass you when they should and the clubface will stay

Photo 41: The correct head position.

open, pushing, slicing, or shanking your ball.

Tiger Wood's head is over his back toe at impact, which creates a powerful unleashing action with the club at impact. *Photo 41* shows the correct

Photo 42: Head and upper body
are too far forward.

head position. My right ear and head are still behind the ball as I strike it, and only move up and through after the ball is gone. My arms, hands, and

club did all they were supposed to because my head stayed back though impact.

The player in *Photo 42* has moved her head and upper body too far forward. Her arms and club are pushing out to the left with the clubface wide open because the natural rolling action couldn't happen.

I see this is a problem in nearly every student. Some move their head forward a great deal, while others move only slightly. But, in every case, this faulty position can wreak havoc with your swing. Tour professionals actually move their head back during their downswings, which further adds to their ability to hit the ball so far. As their head moves back, it increases their arm speed, which increases their clubhead speed. They drive their lower bodies through to the target with incredible power, but keep their heads behind the ball, which prevents them from moving their entire body ahead of the ball. A simple thought would be this. At impact, your head is in the same position it was at address.

To recap this entire chapter: You begin your downswing with your legs starting the downward motion. Whatever you think of, be it zipper, hips, knees, or right shoulder, what you move first is your lower body. This turning motion through the ball shifts your weight from your left leg over to your right leg and pulls your arms and club down last.

At impact, you're up slightly on your left toe, and your zipper is already pointing in front of the ball. The top of your follow through should find your body facing the target, with your knees touching and your left toe in a vertical position.

If someone were to ask what your arms did on your downswing you should say, "I have no idea." You don't want to know. Your arms move much too fast for you to have any influence on them. They swing though the ball because your body pulled them. If your friend watches you swing and says, "you're not rolling your wrists, or turning the club over at impact," just run away screaming. You can't manipulate the hands and club on the downswing, it happens too fast.

A final thought on this comes from the book, The *Search for the Perfect Swing*. A test was conducted with golfers hitting balls indoors into a net. The golfers were told that the lights would be turned out at some point in their swing, and they were to stop if they could. It was a special light that went instantly dark. What the scientists wanted to discover was at what point the golfers could not stop, or what was the point of no return. What they found was that all the golfers could stop if the lights went off during their backswing, but none of them could stop if the downswing had started by even an inch. Once you have started your downswing there's nothing you can do about it, so these thoughts of rolling your wrists are futile. The authors stated, "The time the downswing takes (0.2 - 0.25 seconds) is just about the minimum time required for the brain to perceive external signals, to give orders for the appropriate action, and for the muscles concerned to do something about it. Should a golfer feel he has "gone wrong" at any stage after his downswing has started, there is absolutely nothing he can do about it."

The book goes on to say that the backswing can be corrected easily but any corrections the player may try to make in his downswing, have to be thought about before the downswing actually begins. If you want to do something during your downswing, you needed to be thinking about it at your address or during your backswing.

I hope these findings add to your understanding of just how important your stance, handshake, and wall are. If these fundamentals are correct, and you swing back well, you will come down correctly. The slingshot analogy holds true for you again. Pull the rubber band back correctly and it can only shoot through, right on target.

Chapter Six:
The Top of the Swing

Chapter Six: The Top of the Swing

Chapter Three taught you the handshake move. This fundamental got your club back to waist high, in the correct position, and got you turning your shoulders along the way. In my teaching, it's the most important move in your golf swing. In your practice sessions, you may have gone a bit past the waist high position. That's fine. The momentum of your swing naturally does this. Now, let's look at what you should intentionally do to reach the top.

Is there a correct position at the top of the swing? Is there a wrong one? Do the Tour pros reach the top in the same way? The answer to all these questions is "not really." The Three Fundamentals, (handshake, wall, and zipper) were based on what virtually all Tour pros did the same way, without exception. In my analysis, the top of the swing showed differences from one pro to the next. While many of them were similar, they were not exactly the same. Nicklaus had his arms and club in one position, while Ben Hogan swung to the top in a drastically different way. Fred Couples, Tiger Woods, and Lee Trevino were also different from the others. There really wasn't a model position where they were the same. They all did the wall and the handshake, but only a handful looked the same at the top. In my own teaching, it's the one part of the swing that I spend the least amount of time on. I've always felt that if ten Tour pros reached the top of the swing ten different ways, it isn't nearly as important as the three fundamentals.

This is not to say that any way you reach the top is going to be correct. It

Photo 43: An upright plane.

simply implies that there is a broad range of acceptable ways to get there. With the vast majority of my own students, I have found that if they get to their handshake position correctly, they tend to be fine at the top. Starting their swing back in the correct fashion gets them to the top correctly as well. On the other side of the coin, if they initially start the club back incorrectly, they arrive in a position at the top that makes hitting the ball intensely difficult. Many students have heard terms like "plane" or "path" and are concerned that they should do the right thing. The "plane" and "path" of the golf swing are characteristics that may be looked at and can be discussed in great detail. However, for most of us, they take care of themselves if the handshake is done correctly. The plane of your swing is greatly influenced by your height and posture. Two golfers with different physical make-ups will have different planes. I sure think that "handshake" is easier to think of than "plane" and having one less thing to worry about isn't all bad.

Photo 43 shows a golfer with a very upright swing, meaning her arms and club are very high at the top. This would be an upright plane. Most tall golfers tend to have upright positions at the top of their swing simply

Photo 44: A "flat" swing.

because they have long arms, legs, and torsos. *Photo 44* shows what is called a flat swing, with the golfer's club being lower to the ground. A golfer of shorter stature usually has a flatter swing. Ben Hogan had an extremely flat swing, as opposed to Jack Nicklaus, who was as upright as it gets. These two gentlemen couldn't be further apart at the top of their swings, yet both were correct, and their respective positions served them well. Because their body types were differ-

ent, where they arrived at the top of their swings was also different. If Nicklaus tried to copy Hogan, he wouldn't have had anywhere near the success he did.

Photo 45: "Crossing the line."

Fred Couples has a unique position at the top of his swing, which bears talking about. Couples "crosses the line" at the top but still manages to hit the ball as solidly as anyone does. *Photo 45* shows what crossing the line is. Instead of the golfer's club pointing at the target at the top of the swing, the clubhead points off to the left. Many golfers that tend to over-swing get their club in this position. With the club pointing off to the left at the top, it needs to be rerouted on the down-swing to find the ball squarely. This requires the golfer to have an extra move in his swing, but as Couples clearly shows, the "crossed line position" is not wrong, it's just harder to

Photo 46: The club is "laid off."

duplicate.

Some of us have our clubhead pointing off to the right when it's at the top. This is called having the club "laid off," as seen in *Photo 46*. Again, an adjustment is required, at some point in the swing, to let the clubface strike the ball squarely. But being "laid off" cannot be considered wrong either, just harder to repeat.

Photo 47: The ideal position.

What both Tour pros and instructors consider "correct" is to have the clubhead pointing directly at the target when it reaches the top of the swing. The shaft of the club is parallel to the target line, like it was at the handshake position. *Photo 47* shows what could be considered ideal. A 90-degree angle is formed with the two arms and the left elbow point down to the ground. Most professionals keep their left elbow from getting too high (moving away from their body), preventing what in golf terms is called a "flying elbow." If the elbow flies away, the golfer then needs to drop it back down against his body to start the downswing to prevent the dreaded "over the top move." In my experience, if my student has the club parallel to his toes at the handshake position (waist high in the backswing), 90% of them have the club parallel when they reach the top. I definitely feel they'll have an easier chance of making solid contact when they come down. But if they're off a little at the top I don't worry too much about it. You don't hit the ball at the top of your swing; you hit it at the bottom. I can swing up to the top of my swing and twirl the club around my head three times and still hit a good shot if I want to, and have shown this to my students many times. An exaggeration to be sure, but if your clubface comes into the ball squarely and with a lot of power, the top of your swing should be the least of your concerns.

From the waist-high handshake position the arms and club will go up. After your right shoulder has turned 90 degrees, your body's job is done. You don't really have to keep turning unless you're naturally flexible. From here, simply allow your arms and club to keep going on their own. They go up and end in a position that's over your left shoulder. The club is cocked 90 degrees in relation to your right arm. You don't purposely cock it up. It just does it due to the momentum. If you went to the top of your swing and stopped, then dropped the shaft of the club down, it would hit the outside edge of your shoulder. The club doesn't want to hit your head, nor does it want to miss your shoulder all together. From this position, returning to the ball squarely is a much easier proposition.

Photo 48: The young player above has a "cupped" right wrist instead of the correct flat right wrist, as in Photo 47.

One final note about the top. Remember how we wanted the label of your glove pointing out, not up, when you were in your handshake position? Well, at the top of your swing, your right wrist should be flat, as in *Photo 47*, and not cupped, as in *Photo 48*. When the right wrist is cupped, you open your clubface and squaring it up may be difficult when you swing down. This is not a must for you. There have been many great players with a cupped wrist, but keeping it flat is simply easier. Sometimes a student may cup his right wrist only with

his driver and doesn't with his irons. The length of the driver contributes greatly in this, so be careful when you pick up the driver.

In summary, the top of your swing is something that just happens after the club is swung through the handshake position. The centrifugal force applied to the club, as is moves through waist high, automatically carries it to the top. The position the club is in at the waist high position is crucial to its reaching a successful position at the top. The club may be square, high, low, laid off, or may even cross the line at the top. All of these may still produce effective shots but, as mentioned above, some may require additional moves to accomplish this during the downswing. With the club pointing "down the target line," the golfer doesn't have to worry how his club will come down. There are, in fact, four different times that your club is parallel to your target line.

A) During your handshake when the club is waist high.

B) At the top, when the clubhead points at the target.

C) At waist high on the downswing, when the club is in the same position it was during the handshake on the backswing.

D) At waist high on the follow-through, when your left hand "shakes hands," the shaft of the club is again parallel to the target line.

Chapter Seven:
Bad Shots and How to
Correct Them Yourself

Chapter 7: How to Correct Your Bad Shots

The job of any teacher, in any profession, is to teach the student to be able to teach him or herself. In golf, being able to make on course corrections on your own is essential. It definitely keeps your blood pressure down.

We're going to look at the most common bad shots, and what to look for in your swing so you can correct them without too much trouble. All the solutions are found in the preceding chapters, but presenting them to you in a "quick-correct" format will help you fine-tune your analytical skills. If an answer is confusing to you, go back and reread the appropriate chapter for a more in-depth explanation.

A pull to the right.

A) Shoulders may be open, aiming you right to begin with. Check your "tilt."

B) Ball position may be too forward. By the time your club reaches the ball, it's closed. Remember the "one-half inch" rule.

C) You're on your toes. If your body senses it's leaning out over the ball during the swing, it automatically swings up and around you on the downswing to pull you back up. Distribute your weight more evenly.

D) Your club may be starting back outside the target line. Your hands may be taking the club back without turning your shoulders. Going back outside on the backswing makes the club pull inside on the downswing, guaranteeing a pull. Go to your handshake.

E) You may have knocked your wall over. Too much weight went over to your left leg so you couldn't drive your legs through first on your downswing. This makes your club arrive at the ball too soon, hitting the ball off to the right. Keep your wall solid.

F) No zipper turn. Probably caused by knocking your wall over. Without the leg drive, the club and arms pass you on the downswing.

G) You're aiming too far to the left.

A push to the left.

A) Your alignment is off to the left. Most lefthanders aim left of the target. Check your aim by laying a club at your feet. It must be parallel to your target line.

B) Your ball position may be too far back. Your club can't square up in time because the ball is too close to your left foot.

C) Your handshake is going around you too much. Instead of the club being parallel to your toes, it's wrapped around you to the inside when it's half way back, and the hole in your grip is pointing way left. It should point at the target.

D) The label of your glove has turned skyward. Make sure the label points out, not up.

E) Your head is moving forward (toward the target) too much on your downswing. Keep your head back through impact with your right ear over the ball.

A fat shot.
(Hitting the ground before the ball)
A) You knocked your wall over.

With too much weight swaying outside your left leg, you simply can't get your body back where it started. Your club hits into the ground behind the ball where your center of gravity is.

B) You picked the club up too steeply with your arms. If your club goes up too steeply, it comes down too steeply and digs into the ground. Make sure you're turning your shoulders on the backswing.

Hitting thin or topping the ball.

A) Your left leg is straightening as you swing back. Keep the flex in your left leg.

B) You're standing up. Maintain your spine angle during the backswing. Remember, picking your head up is not the problem.

Hooking to the right.

A) Your clubface is closed at impact. Ninety-nine per cent of the time this is because your grip is too strong. Get your hands in a more neutral position to prevent the hands from rolling over too early.

B) The label on your glove may be pointing to the ground during your handshake. The label must face out.

A slice.

A) Shoulders may be open at address. The club swings down where your shoulders are aligned, cutting across the ball putting slice spin on it. Watch your tilt.

B) Ball position may be too far forward. By the time the club hits the ball it's going back toward the right, which also slices across the ball.

C) Only your arms swing back. This out-to-in swing path slices across the ball on the downswing. Make sure

your shoulders are turning.

D) The label of your glove is pointing skyward at the handshake position, opening the clubface. Point the label out, not up.

E) The club is going around you on the backswing too much. The clubface opens and stays open as you swing through. This usually results in a push, but a slice is also possible.

F) Your right wrist is cupped at the top of your swing. Keep the right wrist flat.

G) You're not getting your legs and zipper through on the downswing. An inadequate leg drive keeps the arms and clubface from rolling through enough on the downswing, leaving the clubface wide open.

H) The left hand is not shaking hands on the follow through. Make sure your left hand does its job. If you wear a watch on your left hand, make sure the face "faces out," not down, at waist high on your follow through.

I) Your head may be moving forward again. Keep your head behind the ball through impact.

No power or distance.

A) You're not getting enough shoulder turn on the backswing. This is the number one problem for amateur golfers. Turn, turn, turn. Try for 90 degrees or more.

B) You're not getting your lower body involved on your downswing. Turn your zipper to start your downswing and make sure you end up on your left toe.

A shank.

A) You're on your toes. Getting out on your toes moves your head and clubface out toward the ball too much.

Instead of hitting the sweet spot, you hit the ball off the neck of the club. Stay back over your heels and wiggle your toes.

B) During your handshake, your club is again going around you too much. This thrusts the clubhead out too much on the downswing, striking the ball on the neck.

C) The label of your glove is pointing skyward at the handshake position. If the label points up too much, the clubface stays open at impact and hits the ball of the neck.

D) Your left shoulder is out toward the target line too much at address. Make sure you have enough tilt so the left shoulder is back and lower than the right shoulder.

F) The left hand is not shaking hands. If the left hand doesn't roll over enough and the left palm stays pointing skyward, the clubface will be wide open.

G) Your head is moving forward again. If your head moves forward, your arms thrust out too much and you hit the ball off the neck.

There are, of course, many more faults and remedies that can be apparent in a golf swing. This list of corrections will start you off on improving your analytical skills and allow you to begin to understand your own swing more thoroughly. When you are in the middle of a round and can correct your own bad shots at a moment's notice, and salvage the remaining holes, I know you'll enjoy your game more. If you still can't quite figure out what's causing some of those poor shots, a visit to your pro will "right your ship."

Chapter Eight:
The Short Game

Chapter 8: The Short Game

After learning the elements of your full swing and assembling them into a solid, consistent motion, your ball striking should improve by leaps and bounds. You'll have to spend some quality time on the range perfecting everything, but at least now you know what to work on.

The previous chapters gave you a plan to follow and tools to diagnose your own shots.

The next big step for you is to have a solid short game. The short game encompasses putting, chipping, pitching, bunker play and all those little shots around the green. Research has shown us that two thirds of all golf shots are less than 100 yards from the green. Of those, 43% are putts. It makes absolutely no difference how far you hit the ball if you can't get the ball on the green and into the hole effectively.

Average players simply don't hit as many greens as the pros do, so their short game must be called upon to save them more frequently. This chapter covers the entire short game, and is the lesson that most quickly lowers your score. It may take some time to hit the golf ball 300 yards, but making a 10-foot putt or executing a 30-foot chip will be in your repertoire in no time.

Putting

Once you've spent some time working on your three fundamentals, and your ball striking has improved, it's time to make the putt. Rifling an approach shot right at the pin, then missing the six-foot putt, can be frustrating to anyone who plays this game.

Good putting has always been the backbone of good scoring, and any tournament you watch on TV shows you this on a weekly basis. The player who wins is the one who putts the best, end of story. Your ability to hit fairways and greens is very important, but making the putt completes the job.

Putting styles are as varied as hairstyles. Weaving through the vast array of information out there to arrive at a putting style that is best for you should be your number one job. Should you putt like Nicklaus, or does Tiger's method seem better? Did Hogan have the answer, or does Phil Mickelson's style seem more fundamentally correct? The answer is all these players have developed a method that works for them, and we can learn from all that experience.

Chapter one told you of how the three fundamentals came to be. They were the three positions that every Tour professional did the same way in the swing. I came to my conclusions about putting using the same method: years of observation and personally talking to the Tour pros.

With putting, there were really no positions that *all* of them did the same. But there were several common elements that *most* seemed to share. I studied the putting of players from all the three major Tours, along with the thousands of low handicap amateurs. Then, I assembled a model that averaged out what they all shared in their putting strokes and stances. I call it the "fundamental putt."

Almost all of my students improved dramatically when putting this new way, and felt very comfortable doing so. Even though there are endless variations that are acceptable, this method, more than anything, just makes sense.

The Grip

I teach what is called the "reverse overlap grip," which is without a doubt the grip used by most Tour players. I add a slight change from what is traditionally shown to students, and will explain why I feel it can make you even more solid. *Photo 49* shows the golfer using the "reverse

Photo 49: Reverse overlap grip.

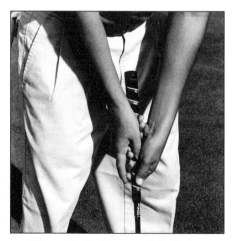

Photo 50: Point your right index finger straight down

overlap" method.

Grip your putter with all ten fingers, like you would hold a baseball bat. Your thumbs rest on top of the putter, not on either side. Now, without moving any other fingers, point your right index finger straight down and have it on the outside of your other fingers, as in *Photo 50*.

Slide your hands closer together now, so they're touching. Place the tip of your right index finger on your left index fingernail. All nine of your fingers are touching the club, and your right index finger is outside the other fingers.

I call this your trigger finger. Your feeling, power, control, and pressure point are all in your trigger finger, much like squeezing the trigger of a gun. Having your trigger finger in this position gives you a very stable, controlled grip on your putter. You now push the putter back with your trigger finger. Your putter can swing back freely without having the wobble that is common to so many players.

The main reason your trigger fin-

Photo 51: Right wrist is flat when you strike the ball.

ger is helpful is that it keeps your right hand and wrist in control during the stroke, and prevents your left hand from overtaking the right. With the right index finger in control, the back of your right hand stays in a constant position during the stroke, and eliminates the right wrist from cupping during the downswing. The right wrist is flat at address and should remain flat as you strike the ball. *Photo 51* shows this clearly. The golfer's hands have

Photo 52: A cupped right wrist.

stayed in the same position all the way through the stroke. *Photo 52* shows a golfer "breaking down" during her stroke. The right wrist has cupped significantly, which is always going to result in a missed putt. Cupping the right wrist usually results in a pull to the right, because the head of the putter passes your hands too early. Your goal is to keep your hands ahead of the putter head.

Instead of your hands fighting each other for control during the stroke, the trigger finger grip lets your two hands operate as one. Blending your hands together lets you swing the putter back and through in a smooth, controlled motion.

The standard reverse overlap grip is nearly identical, with one exception. Instead of the right index finger being on the left fingernail, many professionals have it curled up slightly. The right finger is still outside the other fingers, but instead of it being straight down as far as it will go, it's curled up a bit and rests near the second and third fingers of your left hand, as in *Photo 49*. This is fine as well, and is especially good for golfers with smaller hands. Many of you will find that it's impossible, or uncomfortable, to get the right finger all the way down to the left finger nail. Curling it up may be better for you. I've always felt that the further down you can get it, the better, because it lets your right hand stay in control longer. However, use the one that is most comfortable for you.

One last point: grip pressure. This advice may also sound new or different to what you've heard in the past, but it happens to be true. You've read or heard you should grip the putter as lightly as you can, or have it just laying in your hands. This is supposed to enhance your feel during your stroke. In most cases, Tour professionals hold the putter quite firmly. On a scale of one to 10, I'd say their grips were a seven. It makes sense really. If your grip is firm, it keeps the putter from twisting during your stroke. It firms up your wrists and keeps your arms out of the stroke. A gentle grip is necessary on a full swing. It adds to your power because your arms and wrists release through the shot. But on a putt accuracy is your number one goal. I don't really care what the old wives' tale is. The pros squeeze that putter pretty darn tight.

Putting Cross-handed

Gripping the putter with your right hand lower than your left became "the thing to do" in the 1980's, and has helped thousands of golfers make more putts. Fred Couples is a good example of a cross-handed putter who has had great success. More and more golfers are going cross-handed, and there can be no denying their success in getting the ball in the hole. Johnny Miller said that if golf were invented all over again, pros would start teaching cross-handed right from day one. Cross-handed does much the same that the trigger finger grip does. It puts the right hand in a dominant position, preventing the left hand from taking over.

Photo 53: The cross-handed grip.

It makes the right wrist flat, and lets it stay flat throughout the stroke. *Photo 53* shows the cross-handed style.

I have found, however, that most golfers who putt cross-handed do so because they couldn't putt very well the traditional way. They tried and tried but nothing seemed to work, so they ended up cross-handed. What is usually the case is that they were never shown the reverse overlap grip (trigger finger grip) and their gripping style

caused many problems. New students of mine arrive for their putting lesson putting cross-handed, and leave using the traditional method once I have shown them the trigger finger. Most golfers simply feel more comfortable using the traditional style. It makes sense, because you grip all your other clubs with the left hand lower than the right. With their new trigger finger grip, I show them the rest of the putting address and stroke, and the vast majority of them improve significantly. I think the cross-handed method is great and may be the style of the future. But first, try the methods outlined in the rest of the chapter. It will work for you too.

The Arms

Hang your arms down straight during your address position, with little or no bending in your elbows. By simply bending at the waist a little (10 degrees) your arms will hang down naturally. When you grip the putter, your triangle is present. With your arms in this position there's very little bending of your elbows or wrists, which eliminates many angles that can cause inconsistency.

Some of you may be thinking that Nicklaus and Palmer look nothing like this at address. They're all hunched over and have their elbows sticking out. Their wrists are cupped and they don't have the triangle. Jack and Arnie are two of the greatest putters the game has ever seen. I can't think of too many other guys I'd rather have putting to save my life than these two. What's going on? Why shouldn't you putt like them? Well, let me give you some reasons.

First of all, putting used to be

taught that way. When Jack and Arnie learned the game, their style was generally taught wherever you went for lessons. Secondly, the greens that players of this era played on were much slower than what you find today. The early '70s found tremendous advances in greenskeeping, with new grasses being developed. Greens from past generations were quite slow and required a real 'hit' with the putter to get the ball to go anywhere. Lining up with the elbows and wrists all flared out, produced a "wristy" stroke that could get the ball all the way to the hole.

Lastly, these two gentlemen, along with other great players in their era have a tremendous amount of talent. They could probably stand on their head and putt backwards and still make their putt. Their style demanded a great deal of practice. They spent countless hours grooving their strokes. And, they got paid to putt well.

With the introduction of modern greens, putts now roll much faster and smoother than they use to, so a putting stroke that is smooth as well seems to make sense. Nicklaus has taken much of the wristiness out of his stroke, and today's players look "silky" when they putt. Having your elbows flared out too much, having too much wrist cup, and breaking down the triangle, simply creates too many moving parts for most of us to handle. Venturi calls things like this, "unnecessary angles." Isn't it easier to have fewer, rather than more angles in your stance and swing?

Hanging your arms down straighter eliminates many of these angles and promotes a more pendulum-like motion when your putt. On today's Tour, you see fewer and fewer pros all

Photo 54: The ideal putting stance.

bent over and more players standing taller to their putt. It might take some time for you to adjust to the change, but stay with it for a while and I think you'll enjoy your newfound success.

Ball Position
Play the ball forward in your stance, off your right heel. It's close to where you play the ball when setting up to hit a driver. Anywhere from an inch inside your right heel to directly off your right toe is fine. Ben Crenshaw and Phil Mickelson play their ball about an inch forward of their big toe. The tip of your trigger finger should point down directly to your ball position. This is a great way

to check this position. Your ball should be where your right index finger points. Playing the ball from this position lets the putter strike the ball when it should, right at the bottom of your arc. If the ball is played too far back in your stance, your putter hits it with too steep a descending blow, which could cause the ball to hop. If the ball is too far forward, you may catch it on the upswing and only give it a glancing blow. Play around with it some to determine the ideal position for your stroke.

Eyes over the Ball

You should be close enough to the ball at address so that your eyes are directly over the line of the ball. They're behind the ball a few inches, since the ball is played well forward, but are on the same line. If you stand too far away at address, your eyes fall on a line that is inside the ball too much. This makes it harder to see and feel the line, and usually causes a push. You also never want to stand so close that your eyes are outside the ball looking back in at it. This is quite the rarity, but I've seen it. You can check if your eyes are over the ball with the following drill.

Assume your address position. Now, hold a ball up on top of your nose, or right between your eyes. When you drop the ball, it should strike the ground right on the line of your ball. Again, it may hit slightly behind the ball itself, but it's on the line and that's what's important.

The Stance

Most good putters address the ball with a square to slightly open stance. Some have their feet on a parallel line, while many others stand about 10 degrees open with their right leg pulled back off the line slightly. I think either of these is fine, but I tend to lean more toward the 10-degree open stance. Standing slightly open lets you see the line a little better and gets your right leg out of the way of your arms. What you never want to do is stand closed. Aiming your feet and body to the left of the hole is never going to produce a good putt, much the same as it would never produce a good shot on your full swing. It's a tendency some players have, but it not what you want. Billy Casper stood from a closed position and putted with great success, but he's the only one I've ever seen.

Also, put about 10% more weight on your right leg at address. This slight lean toward the hole encourages a stable lower body during the stroke and keeps you from scuffing the putter into the ground on the backswing. You start with 60% of your weight on your right leg at address and it stays there throughout the stroke. There is no shifting back and through.

Summary of Putting Address

1. Align your feet parallel to the target line or slightly open at address. Most good golfers do.

2. Position the ball forward, almost off your right toe. Your trigger finger points at the ball.

3. Hang your arms down so there's little or no bending in your elbows. You'll bend from the waist about 10 degrees.

4. Have a flat right wrist.

5. Have your eyes over the ball.

The golfer in *Photo 54* looks ideal.

The Putting Stroke

Just as there are countless varieties of putting stances, putting strokes are as varied as the day is long. In this section I'm going to show you what my own students have had great success with, and tell you what most good putters do on their strokes.

1. Take a relatively short backswing. You're only rolling the ball across the green, so a big backswing is not necessary. Too much backswing is the most common error I see in amateurs. By taking the putter back too far, the chances of it squaring up are greatly reduced. Mentally, if you take too much backswing, your brain is going to say, "Uh-oh, this is going to go too far." This forces you to slow down your swing through the ball, which will never produce a crisp hit. Decelerating your putter is going to lead to an off-line, sloppy putt that will never find the bottom of the hole.

2. Swing the putter head through, toward the hole to follow through. A thought I use in every lesson is, "point the putter at the hole." If your putter points toward the target, the ball will roll toward the target. It's as simple as that. You want to feel like you're putting the head of your putter in the hole, like you're chasing after the ball. Along with making the ball roll toward the hole, this thought also gets your focus off the ball and puts it more in your stroke. Your goal is to swing the putter, not hit the ball. When you have a short putt to win the hole you can't help but be a little nervous. Instead of putting pressure on yourself to roll the ball into the cup, the thought of pointing the putter into the hole eliminates the feeling of having to hit the ball.

Another analogy I use is pretending you're holding a 3-foot long flashlight. The light shines out of the head of the putter. During your stroke, simply shine the light into the hole. If the light shines into the hole, the ball will find its way there too.

With too much backswing, you'll be afraid to do any of this because your ball will roll too far. Keep the backswing to a minimum, just don't get quick or jerky.

3. Don't break your wrists during your putting stroke. Wrists supply power in the golf swing. You don't need power when you're putting. You need accuracy. Keeping the wrists firm also eliminates excessive opening and closing of the putter head. The chances of keeping the putter blade square during your stroke will greatly increase if

Photo 55: Keep right wrist flat throughout putt.

your wrists aren't flipping all over the place. The putting swing is a miniature version of the triangle swing. Your triangle is present at address, and it should stay together during the whole stroke. It's there on your full swing, and is most certainly there when you putt.

Your right arm, and wrist in particular, stay firm throughout the stroke. The right wrist should be flat as you address your putt, and should stay flat as you swing. As we mentioned in the putting address section, your right wrist should never bend up or cup, as you swing your putter through toward the hole. Ben Crenshaw and Phil Mickelson demonstrate this most clearly in their strokes. See *Photo 55*.

3. Your lower body should remain completely still during your stroke. Too often the golfer moves his legs back and through when he putts. That makes the putter return inconsistently into the ball. The power that the lower body creates is crucial when trying to hit the ball 300 yards, but in putting it shouldn't move. Your triangle simply moves back and through, with the legs remaining still.

4. Now here's a big one. One of the most debated subjects in this game is on what path your putter should swing as you putt. Should your putter head swing straight back and through, or should it swing back slightly to the inside on the backswing, then return to square as you hit the ball. Half the people teaching this game believe it should be straight. The other half is just as adamant swinging back and inside. Both methods have their supporters and in most cases nothing you say can change their opinion.

I teach the method that lets the putter head swing back inside the target line on the backswing, and return to square at impact. The putter hits the ball then moves back inside on the follow through. Why do I teach and believe in this theory?

I have rarely, if ever, seen a Tour pro who swings his putter back straight. Maybe on a 6-inch putt, but

only then. I believe that if the best golfers in the world all do it this way, it is probably right.

The explanation I give to my own students is a bit long. Please bear with me. If you hold a croquet mallet, you

Photo 56: Putter shaft is 15 degrees off vertical.

would see that the handle, or shaft, comes up at a 90-degree angle. You straddle the line with one foot on either side of the ball and swing through. The mallet head swings straight back on the backswing and swings straight on the downswing. It has to.

Golf clubs are not made straight up and down like this. The golfer stands off to the side of the ball and the shaft of the club angles out. Remember the "lie of the club?" The shaft is not vertical; it's angled down some. Most standard putters have a lie of about 75 degrees. The grip is some 15 degrees off of vertical. See *Photo 56*.

Because of this lie, and because

Photo 57: Putter swings back like the outer edge of a door.

you stand off to the side of the ball, the putter must swing in like a door swings. If you hold a putter against a door, then open the door, the head of the putter swings back inside. It looks like the toe of the putter is opening as the door swings open, but in reality, it's swinging back square. The door you're opening will close squarely every single time you swing it back and through. The edge of the door swings back and the hinges of the door don't move. It's impossible for the edge of the door to swing back straight since the hinges are staying still. The only way for the door to swing back on line would be if the hinges were on the top of the door instead of the side. See *Photo 57*.

Since you're standing to the side of the ball, and the putter head is out away from you, the putter must swing back to the inside.

Another way to visualize this is to put the grip of your putter up under your chest and choke your arms down. You're creating your triangle. When you're bent over and turn back (*Photo 58*), the head of the putter swings back

Photo 58: Putter swings around you.

slightly inside or around you. It returns to square at impact, then closes, or moves to the inside on the follow through. Ben Crenshaw and Phil Mickelson are two of the best at swinging the putter back naturally, inside.

Trying to artificially swing the putter straight back leads to a movement of your putter that cuts across your putt or pulls it right of the hole. Going back dead straight is actually going back outside the line, and goes against what is "natural." I see many students whose putters go back outside their line on the backswing, then hit their ball right of the hole every time. Unless they do some split second adjustments on their downswing, and

*Photo 59: Eliminating the
"cut stroke" drill.*

open up the head of their putter just before impact, they're going to miss it every time.

Here is an easy drill to for you to try to stop this "cut stroke."

Line up to your putt and lay an extra club down just outside the toe of your putter. Make sure this club is parallel to your target line, as in *Photo 59*. With this club lying on the ground, swing your putter back. The toe of your putter should move slightly away from the club as it swings back. If you take the putter back straight, you'll notice that the head of your putter is swinging back and going out over the top of this club. You may even bump into it as you go back. Laying this club on the ground instantly shows you that your putter is going back outside the line. What you thought was straight isn't. Spend ten minutes doing this on the practice green and your putting is sure to improve.

The design of your putter also influences your ability to swing back correctly.

Where the shaft of your putter connects to the head may make it easier or more difficult to achieve this inside to inside path. A putter that has the shaft connected right on the heel makes it easier to have an inside stroke. Since the shaft goes into the heel of the putter, it lets the putter head swing more to the inside when you take the putter back.

Some putters have the shaft connected more toward the middle of the head. While there are many putters that have this feature, mentally, and optically, this putter seems like it wants to swing back straight. This putter is ideal for the player who tends to swing back too far inside the target line. Getting your professional to fit you with a putter that is best for you would be time well spent on your part.

The chapter on club fitting will explore this further, just keep in mind that different people "see the line" differently, and having a putter that is right for you is crucial in your success.

The Grain

When watching golf on TV, quite often you hear the announcer say, "The grain got that one." What they are talking about is the way the grass grows, or lays. Grass doesn't grow straight up; it lays one way or another. The way you part your hair is an example. You may brush it to the left or to the right, but rarely do you brush it straight up.

Reading the grain is an important factor in becoming a good putter because the grain has a direct influence on how your ball rolls. Reading the grain becomes more important as your putting abilities improve, since your stroke and speed become more refined. A beginning golfer misses his putt because he simply didn't hit it right, but a Tour pro usually has a very good stroke. The professional can line up correctly, grip the putter correctly, and swing his putter very well, so reading the grain becomes quite important to him. Work on your stance and swing every day, so you can trust it. When you're confident of your putting abilities, then focus some on the grain.

How you determine the grain is not difficult when you know what to look for. Here are the basic guidelines that I give my students.

1. Grass grows toward the sun and grows stronger toward the setting sun. There is usually no debate among golf professionals when it comes to this tip. Anything living, (grass, flowers, trees, etc.) needs energy to grow, and the sun is energy. Early in the morning, as the sun is rising in the east, the grass on the green lays a bit in that direction. Then from noon each day, until the sun sets, the sun is in the western sky. The grass on the green is trying to reach up toward it when it grows. Most of the day, the sun is in the west, and its energy pulls everything toward it.

I asked our greens superintendent one day if this means that the grain will grow east if you're playing at 8:00 a.m., and he said "sort of." He explained that the sun isn't high enough, or strong enough yet to pull the grain all the way over to the east. The sun is too low and isn't hitting the Earth at an angle where it will have enough influence on the grass. The grass may lay a bit to the east early in the morning, but it never totally lays

down that direction. During the course of the day the grain follows the sun as it moves from east to west, but it is laying west during a larger portion of the day.

Now, what do you do if you can't see the sun, like on a cloudy day, or the sun is straight up when you're playing at lunchtime? There's a trick that most Tour pros use, which can show you the grain in about two seconds.

Stand in the middle of the green and look down while turning around the whole green. Some of the green will look dull, or deep green, while the other side will look white or shiny. When you see the shine, that's the way the grain is going. The grass is laying down away from you when you see the shine, so putting toward the shine is going down grain. Your ball will roll a bit faster since there's less resistance from the grass. If you turned around and putted toward the 'dull' looking part of the green you'd be putting into the grain and your ball will roll much slower. The ball is rolling into the edges of the grass and is meeting resistance.

The way I remember shiny versus dull is: "Shiny, like glass." When you're putting with the shine, it will be like rolling your ball down a glass top on a coffee table…fast! Be most aware of the shine when you're putting down hill. A downhill, down grain putt will be like rolling your ball down the hood of your car.

If you have an uphill putt, you know it will be a bit slower. If it's also against the grain, you're really going to have to give it a good whack. On either of these two putts remember that the grain will affect the ball even more as it slows down nearer the hole.

The ball isn't rolling as fast toward the end of your putt, so it loses much of its velocity. Any grain will start grabbing the ball and influence its roll. The same theory applies to how the ball breaks. The slope of the green will most influence the ball as it nears the hole simply because it's not rolling very fast.

When you're putting across the grain, you must realize how the roll of the ball will also be affected. Let's say you have a putt that will break 12 inches from left to right. If the grain is growing left to right as well, your putt may break 15 inches since it's going with the grain. If the grain was growing toward your left, that same putt may only break nine or 10 inches since it's trying the break into the grain.

The grass in the fairways also has a grain and which way the mowers cut the grass affects which way the grass lays. On many of the holes, instead of the mowers cutting from the tee box toward the green, they mow from the green back toward the tee. Mowing this way makes your drives roll significantly less because the ball is rolling into the grain. The grain also affects pitch shots and your chips. If you have a little chip from off the fringe, it's much more difficult if your club is hitting into the grain. The grass will tend to grab the clubhead if you're chipping into the grain, and won't affect the club as much if you're chipping with the grain. Many times you see the professional on TV bend down and stare at his ball for a while. He's not only seeing if the grass is long or short, but is finding out which way the grain is growing.

Being able to read the grain is not the most important aspect in your golf game, but it can aid you in figuring out how your ball will react.

Chipping

Anywhere from one to ten yards off the green is your chipping zone. Chipping may very well be the biggest factor in instantly reducing your score, and is a skill that can be mastered by everyone who plays this game. I often tell my students that not many people will ever hit 300-yard drives, but we can all chip a ball a few yards onto the green.

Like putting, chipping is a "Great Equalizer." Any golfer of any age can chip as well as a Tour pro. Because it might take you a few more strokes to get near the green, you must chip better than the pros. Tour pros hit an average of close to 75% of the greens, so they chip about four times a round. Most amateurs only hit four greens per round and have to chip 14 times. Good grief, if you need to chip 14 times when you play, you better know how to chip, and be quite good at it. Think about it. If you hit 14 good chip shots up close to the hole and tap the putt in, you've just knocked your three- putt hole down to two, and your two-putt hole down to one. A golfer that's shooting 92 could average 78! With the same woods and irons that you've always hit, if you can chip the ball close to the hole every time, your score will go down into uncharted territory. If you chip the ball to within a few feet of the hole, or actually chip it in, that's perfect and no one on the Tour could do better. You may have flubbed your drive, but if you chip the ball in, that's a par.

Being a good chipper also helps the rest of your game in ways you may not have thought of. If you're back in the fairway 150 yards, and you know you're a good chipper, you'll be less apprehensive about having to hit the green. You feel like you can hit the ball almost anywhere and still be able to make a par because you know you'll chip the ball close. With this confidence going for you, you'll swing better and, in turn, hit the green anyway. Your ball striking improved because you weren't trying to steer your swing so much. You were no longer afraid of missing the green. It really is a snowball affect that can even go back to your tee shot.

Learning to be a good chipper is the fastest, easiest way to lower your score.

Photo 60: "Dig."

Club Selection

I'm going to have you use a 5-7-9 and Sand wedge. These four clubs are all you're ever going to need when you chip. It certainly isn't wrong to use a 6 or an 8, but using only these four, and only practicing with these four, will give you a great deal of confidence. You'll know you have the right club for the job. I would never use less loft than a 5 iron because your ball probably wouldn't even get off the ground. Make the 5 the lowest number you would ever consider. On the other

end of the club selection, notice I said sand wedge, not pitching wedge. Other than the putter, your sand wedge is designed differently than any other club in your bag. Knowing that difference is tremendously important for your game.

Every iron in your bag, except your sand wedge, has the same characteristic in its design (*Photo 60*). If you hold your club with the shaft straight up and down, and look at the bottom of the club, you'll see that the front edge of the club slopes down, or is closer to the ground than the back edge. This is called dig. The leading edge of your irons is designed to dig into the ground

Photo 61: "Bounce."

when you swing, which allows you to take a divot. The bottom of your sand wedge slopes the other way, with the leading edge being higher than the back edge (*Photo 61*). This characteristic is called the bounce. Instead of the club digging into the ground, it now glides through, or bounces as it hits the ball. The club will have a very easy time sliding through the grass instead of getting caught up.

Gene Sarazen invented the sand wedge in the early 1930's. Until that time, hitting out of a bunker was a difficult task even for pros, as the leading edge of their pitching wedge would chunk into the sand. Sarazen came out one day and started popping them out of the bunker with relative ease, and his fellow pros were astounded at his success.

Ken Venturi, who was lifelong friends with Sarazen, tells how Sarazen kept his new sand wedge in his bag upside down for a while, because he didn't want to give away his secret. He wasn't even sure it was legal. We'll cover bunker play later, but you can certainly understand how the bounce has forever changed the game and can make your chipping easier.

The sand wedge is also a heavier club, so it gets through the grass easier. If you have a lob wedge in your bag I think it's even better than a regular sandwedge. A lob wedge is a sandwedge, it just has more loft. Most lob wedges have 60 degrees of loft, (some even have 64) and that simply lets you be more aggressive with your shot without fear of the ball rolling too far. The ball will have more backspin and will stop on the green a bit quicker than a standard sandwedge that has 56 degrees of loft. You don't have to run out and buy one, but it is a club I know you'll use quite often. You can also use your lob wedge to pitch with and hit out of the sand for much the same reason. You can hit it harder, higher and impart more spin on the ball than you can with a standard sandwedge. Keep the lob wedge in mind as you continue through the rest of the short game chapters.

The one time you will use your pitching wedge to chip is off a tight lie. When your ball is sitting on hardpan and there's no cushion of grass under the ball, you'll need the sharp leading edge of your pitching wedge to get under the ball. The bounce on your sand wedge would skull the ball over the green because there is little or no grass for the club to get under. At the Masters Tournament the grass on the fairways and around the greens is cut to an extremely short length, often as short as other courses' greens. Pros often chip with their pitching wedges when at Augusta because tight lies prevail throughout the golf course. You can imagine trying to chip with your sand wedge off a putting green…it's going to be very difficult.

The Golden Rules

Now that we understand club selection, we need to know which of the four clubs to use on a specific shot. "The Golden Rules" were created for just this purpose, and I have taught them throughout my career.

Golden Rule #1

Get the ball on the green as soon as possible. Your goal when you chip is to get the ball on the green and let it roll. A chip shot is simply a putt that goes up in the air first. You don't want a lot of air time on your chips. Anyone can roll a ball on the ground, and getting the ball on the ground sooner will give you better control.

When you go bowling, you throw the ball just over the line, and let it roll all the way down the alley. I don't know any pro bowler that heaves the ball all the way down to the pins. Without a doubt, the biggest mistake I see amateurs make when they chip is hitting the ball too far onto the green and trying to make it stop. For absolutely no reason at all, they'll hit the ball 40 feet in the air and hope it stops. When I see this, I ask my student, "Is there an elephant laying here that I don't see?" They say they're trying to get the ball up. If there's

Photo 61: The"Hula-Hoop."

nothing to go over, then don't go up. You want to use the 'lowest loft possible' when you chip so your ball can get on the green sooner. I would rather use the 5 iron, than the 7 iron, if it were possible. I'd rather use the 7 than the 9, and the 9 instead of the sand wedge. If it's possible. If there is a tree stump in front of you, your 5 iron isn't going to clear it. Your 9 iron may be needed to clear the stump. You want to use the club that will get the ball on the green as soon as possible and still clear any obstacle in front of you.

Golden rule #1: Use the lowest loft possible and, as soon as possible, get the ball on the green and rolling.

Golden Rule #2

When you walk up to your ball, the first thing you should look at is how far it is to the green. How much do you need to go over before landing on the green? This will be the first tool in deciding on what club you're going to need. You want to land the ball on the green since the green is nice and smooth. You don't want to land in the rough unless it's absolutely necessary. Landing your ball one inch onto the green may be a bit risky since you may not hit the exact spot and you'll end up in the rough. Pick a spot about two yards onto the green. *Photo 61* shows what we'll now call the Hula-Hoop. Two yards onto the green is a big Hula-Hoop and that's what you're going to hit.

The good news about this Hula-Hoop is that it's always in the same spot. No matter what club you have, or what hole you're playing, the hoop is two yards onto the green. If you continually practice chip shots at the hoop, you're going to get very good at it. What you're asking yourself to do is hit your ball only a few yards onto the green. You don't need strength, speed or flexibility to do this. That's why you can chip as well as the pros. They all shoot for the Hula-Hoop as well. With the hoop, your ball is only in the air for a short time. It hits the hoop and starts rolling. You don't have to worry about how high to hit the ball, if any wind will blow it off course, or how much the ball will check up when it hits the ground.

Now let's picture a big putting green 100 feet long. There are four holes on this green. One hole is immediately in front of you, some15 feet onto the green. The next hole is 30 feet away. The one after that is 60 feet back, and the last one is 90 feet away. You might think that hitting the hoop every time won't enable you to roll the ball to these different targets, but this is where Golden Rule #3 comes into play.

Golden Rule #2: Hit the hoop and let it roll.

Golden Rule #3

After you know how to hit the ball into the hoop, the next item you look at is how far away is the hole. Is it close to you, or is it all the way on the other side of the green? This is where your four clubs now enter the picture. If the hole is right in front of you, you will chip with your sand wedge. The sand wedge will pop the ball up slightly, land it in the hoop, and will only roll a few feet. The loft on your sand wedge makes the ball go up and down more and doesn't much roll afterwards.

To the next hole, use your 9 iron. Hitting your same Hula-Hoop, the 9 iron shot will roll a few yards further. The 7 iron will go to the third hole, and your 5 iron will be the club that hits the ball all the way to the back of the green. The 5 iron has very little loft and after hitting the hoop rolls a long way.

The magic in this is you will always hit the same hoop with the same swing. The different clubs roll different distances. You don't ever have to alter your swing. Most amateurs don't use this method, and instead do the opposite. They always chip with the same club, and then change their swing to hit the ball different distances. Wherever the hole is cut, they pick up their 9 iron, for example. They swing really easily when the hole is close to them, and they flub it. Their swing gets a bit harder to hit the 9 to the next hole. Then they swing harder still to get the

9 all the way to the last hole! These golfers have one club and many different swings. I don't think anyone has a refined enough touch to consistently pull this off.

Photo 62: The "Hula-Hoop" drill.

If this idea seems novel to you, think about what you do on the range or golf course. You hit your 5 iron farther than your 9 iron don't you? You don't change your swing. Your goal on the golf course is to stand and swing the same way every time. You change clubs to hit different distances. Your 5 iron goes farther than your 7, which goes farther than your 9, which goes farther than your sand wedge. The same principle will apply to your chipping. *Picture 62* shows this. Your consistency will dramatically improve.

Golden Rule #3: Judge your distance, then pick your club. The swing is always the same.

The Chipping Stance

Standing to hit a chip shot is different than standing to hit a full swing. Power is not a key component. Accuracy is. Take time to learn the proper set-up listed below and memorize the key differences.

1. Choke down on the grip. Your left index finger and thumb can be resting on the shaft. The club is very short now, which only makes sense since you're hitting only a short distance.

2. Get your feet close together. With your feet about 6 inches apart, your lower body will stay very stable on your backswing. Pressure is taken off your lower back.

3. Move in closer to the ball so your eyes are nearly over the ball. You'll feel very close to the ball at this point.

4. Turn your stance, (body and feet) 45 degrees open. Instead of standing parallel to the target line,

Photo 63: The chipping stance.

your body is turned to the right half of a turn. This gets your legs out of the way and lets you see the hole better.

5. The ball is positioned off your left toe. Draw a straight line from the inside of your left foot out toward the ball. That's where the ball should be. Having the ball back in your stance all

but guarantees you'll hit the ball cleanly.

6. Set 90% of your weight on your right leg. Leaning toward the green gives you a descending blow and keeps you from hitting the ball fat.

7. Press your hands forward slightly so they're opposite your right thigh. This is called "hands ahead."

Feel free to move an inch or so to get comfortable, but stay pretty close to this position. *Photo 63* shows the proper chipping position.

The Chip Stroke

There are three key principles I discuss with my own students when showing them the chip stroke. I think you can master this in 10 minutes.

1. No wrists. Pretend your wrists are in a plaster cast. Don't break your wrists on your backswing, and don't break them on your follow through. Wrists supply power in the golf swing, and you don't need power to hit the ball only a few feet.

2. Have a smaller backswing and a longer follow through. It should be similar to what you did on your putting stroke.

Most golfers take too much backswing, then stop as they strike the ball. If you take too much backswing your brain says, "Whoa, we're going to hit this too far," and you stop your downswing. Take a smaller backswing, and then follow through longer. I like to say, "point the club at the hoop, or hole." When your club swings up to the follow through, it should be pointing at the hole. This way, you know that you didn't stop at the ball, you swung through it.

Taking too much backswing may also open or close your clubface too much, making it difficult to square it up at contact. How much backswing you need may vary a little from one golfer to the next, but two or three feet is plenty.

3. The third element is not only the

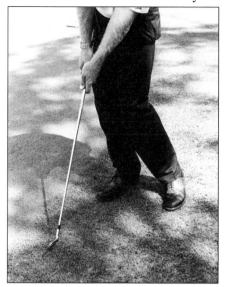

Photo 64: The "knee kick."

most important, but is the one that nobody seems to do naturally. Most golfers I work with seem to have heard they must keep their wrists firm, or to follow through, but hardly any come to the lesson tee doing the third element. To give you a number, I would say in the 35,000 students I have had, maybe 10 of them knew what it was. They all know it now: You must kick in your left knee and heel on your downswing. From your backswing position, your left knee will kick in a bit, starting your downswing. Your knee moves first, and gets to the ball before your club does. Your left heel comes off the ground and inch or two, and the ball is hit with a nice click. (See *Photo 64.*) It doesn't seem like much, but kicking the left knee is the whole ball of wax. Watch most anyone

you play with chip, and you'll notice they never move their left knee, and stay flat-footed during their down-swing. What's going to happen if you don't move your left leg? You'll hit the ball with only your arms. An arm swing will produce a weak, off-line shot that quite often is fat. The grass grabs your club because your arms aren't heavy enough to drive through it.

When you kick your left knee in, you're now using your legs **and** your arms. The club also points more directly at the target, since the legs drove them there. Without the knee kick, your arms and club are working on their own, and may never swing through the same way twice. Sometimes they flip over, causing a pull. Other times they shoot out to the left.

Kicking your left knee in is exactly what you did in Fundamental #3 when you turned your zipper, only in a miniature version. You start your downswing with your lower body when hitting a full shot, and you start it first when you chip. Some Tour pros move their left knee a little, and some a lot, but they all move it. When you try it you'll immediately feel and hear a nice 'click' when you hit the ball. You'll probably hit the first few chips too far until you get used to it, but I assure you, you won't leave them short too often. How much you kick your knee in is what you work on in your practice sessions to develop your touch.

Speaking of touch…I just taught you the technique, and it only takes a few shots to perfect it. I can't teach you touch. You can only refine your touch through practice. How much backswing you take, how much you kick your left knee in, how much you follow through and your ability to hit the Hula-Hoop, can only get better with practice. I would say Tour pros spend 75% of their practice time on their short game, and remember; they only need to chip a few times a round on average. If you need to chip five times as often, shouldn't your practice five times as much? Most of us don't miss a chip 15 or 20 feet off-line, we leave it that much too short or long. Refine your chipping on the practice green by trying to get your balls to be in a three-foot circle around the hole. If your chip rolls to within three feet, you'll have no problem making the putt.

After you've spent some time learning the chip shot, there are some extra little points to master and be aware of to really refine your chipping even further. They are:

A. Try using your putting grip. Your trigger finger grip can aid you in keeping your wrists firm and improve your accuracy. Many professionals chip with their putting grip because it firms up their right wrist considerably.

B. Firm up your grip pressure. Where your grip pressure should be very light in your full swing to help gain clubhead speed and increase power, your chipping grip should be quite firm. Don't squeeze the club until your fingers turn blue, but do be firm enough to prevent the grass from twisting the club off-line.

C. Pretend the ball is on a tee and simply hit the tee. This mental image will let you hit down and not try to scoop the ball up. I like to say, "Use you knee and hit the tee!"

D. Allow the toe of the club to turn over on your follow through. Especially on your 5 and 7 iron shots where the ball runs further, the toe of your club must (naturally) roll over. Artificially trying to keep the clubhead from turning over may push the ball a bit, or even shank the ball because the hosel of the club is coming through first. On chips with your 9 iron or sand wedge, the toe won't close over as much, which will keep a little more loft on the clubhead. You're using the sand wedge because you need the ball to stop, so a little extra loft is only a good thing.

E. If you're in between clubs, go to the higher loft. If there's a hole that could be your 9 iron, but looks like it could also be your 7, use the 9 so you can hit it harder. Selecting the higher lofted club lets you kick your knee in a bit harder so you can be more aggressive and eliminate any chance of a fat shot. If your brain thinks you have too much club, your body may slow down on the downswing because you're afraid to hit it too hard and you'll chunk it. Always be aggressive when you chip.

F. For getting out of ankle-deep rough, forget about the hoop or changing clubs. Long rough requires a very lofted club, like a sandwedge, to get the ball out, and a very hard swing is required. Since you're going to have to swing so hard, the only club you can possibly use will be your sandwedge. A mighty swing with your 5 or 7 iron would send the ball a mile over the green. Since the long rough requires such a big swing, hitting the hoop is nearly impossible to gauge consistently. Only through countless hours of experimentation will you learn how your ball will react out of deep rough.

There are two different ways to play a sandwedge out of deep rough, both of which are covered under the chapter on the playing lesson.

Finally, there is a great practice game you can play to help your chipping to see how you're improving. Most of us, as youngsters, played a basketball game in the driveway called "around the world." You and a friend started right next to the basket and made a short lay-up. If you missed, you had to try it again. Then you moved about 10 feet away and tried that shot. If you missed that one, you had to go back to the beginning and start all over. Eventually, you went to several different spots on the driveway and tried to work your way back around. If at any point you missed one, it was either your friend's turn, or you had to go back and start over. Well, go out to a putting green and go around the whole green.

Get your four chipping clubs, (5-7-9-SW) and your putter. Starting with your sand wedge, chip a ball to the appropriate hole. Then grab your putter and sink the putt. If you miss, you have to go back and chip with the sand wedge again. After you have successfully made the putt, move to where you can chip your 9 iron. Again, try to make the putt. If you make it, you go on to the 7 iron. If you miss, back you go to the sand wedge. See how long it takes you to get up and down with all four clubs without missing a putt. Some of you may do it in 5 minutes, while others may be there for over an hour.

This lets you practice your chipping, changing clubs while chipping, and putting. But more than that, it lets you feel some pressure. You're not playing for a million dollars or anything, but after having spent a half hour getting to the 5 iron, facing a 5-foot putt to finish, or face going back to the sand wedge and doing the whole thing all over again, is quite a daunting task. One day though, you'll face getting up and down with your 5 iron in a tournament situation, and you'll be able to handle the pressure, just like you've done thousands of times on the practice green.

Pitching

Pitching is the third short game element that is crucial in your cutting strokes off your score. You hit a pitch shot when your ball lies some 20 –60 yards off the green. A pitch shot is something like a big chip shot. There are some similarities between the two, but there are subtle differences. Understanding them is important.

A pitch shot is one that has significantly more air time and less roll. Since you're farther away and have more to go over, a higher shot is required. For this reason you're going to use your sand wedge, or lob wedge. The 5-7 and 9 iron can retire for this shot. The loft on your sand wedge will hit the ball high in the air, and let it land on the green with little forward roll. There is no Hula-Hoop concept on pitching. With experience, you'll know how far your sand wedge shot rolls after it lands, and you will pick a spot as close to the hole as possible. This spot changes from one pitch to the next because your distance from the green changes. A twenty-yard pitch requires less power than a 50-yard pitch, and will certainly require less forward roll. It just takes some practice to develop your touch.

If there was ever an oxymoron in this game, it's this. The shot is called a pitch, but I don't want you to use your pitching wedge. Use your sand wedge. Why? The sand wedge has bounce, and the pitching wedge doesn't. The sand wedge will have an easier time getting through the grass because it's not trying to dig in. In my own experience I'd say 90% of amateurs try to pitch with their pitching wedges, and 90% of them either hit it fat, or leave it short of the green. Their pitching wedge digs into the ground and their ball goes about 5 feet. The sand wedge is also heavier and can get through thick rough better.

As I suggested before, when you find yourself on a tight lie, where there's little or no grass beneath the ball, you need the pitching wedge. But that's it. If you don't have a sand wedge you're just killing yourself. Go buy one right now, I'll wait.

The Address Position for Pitching

Now that you have your sand wedge, it's time to learn the pitching set-up. It's similar to chipping, but simply isn't quite the extreme. It is a half shot.

1. Choke half way down on your grip. Since it's a half-shot, have your grip choked down a bit. You don't need the full length of the club to hit a half-shot.

2. Open your stance about 20 degrees. Pulling your right leg back a few inches will get your legs out of the way. The shortened club would jab your torso if you stood square.

3. Put 75% of your weight on your right leg. Setting the weight on the right leg encourages a downward blow so you get the ball up in the air. You're

presetting your weight on the right leg because there's not much time to get it there during the pitching stroke.

4. Play the ball about 2 inches

Photo 65: The pitching stance.

inside your left heel. On chipping, the ball was all the way back, but the pitch is a little inside the heel. Having the ball back in your stance lets you hit the ball before the ground, which keeps you from hitting it fat.

5. Press your hands forward at address so they're in front of your right thigh. This also lets your club swing down a bit steeper so less grass gets between your club and the ball.

6. Feel close to the ball. You can't quite get your eyes over the ball, but at least try to get that "close" feeling. Never reach too far for the ball. *Photo 65* shows a model pitching stance.

The Pitch Stroke

The three elements that were so important in your chip shot are also important to your pitching.

1. No wrists, either back or through. Firm wrists are essential to solid pitching. Your wrists may hinge a little through natural momentum, but don't break them up and down on purpose. Consciously trying to pick the club up on your backswing will only lead to errors on your downswing. The pitch should just be an extension of the chip stroke. Make sure your wrists don't break on the follow through either. Many people are guilty of flipping the wrists up after they hit the ball, trying to artificially create loft. In most cases this results in a thin or topped shot because your club strikes the ball on top. The back of your right wrist should be straight or "flat" and shouldn't ever cup upwards.

2. Have a smaller backswing and a longer follow through. Too much backswing will only scare you into not taking a long follow through. Although every pitch shot is different, your arms and club don't need to go much beyond waist high on your backswing. You're getting into your old handshake position. You've turned your right shoulder back, and your club is parallel to the target line. From this waist high position, you're in no danger of hitting the ball too far, so you can swing through into a nice follow through position. The clubhead hits the ball and continues to swing through toward the target with acceleration. A 60-yard pitch will have more follow through than a 20 yard pitch will, but always swing on through.

Though I see it all too often, the worst possible thing you can do is take a big backswing, cock your wrists up, then swing down and stop the club at the ball, or stick it into the ground. Your swing was slowing down as you approached the ball to keep from hitting it too far.

3. You must kick in your left knee and heel. Again, the movement of your left leg is crucial to the success of your pitch shot. From the top of your backswing, your left leg drives in toward the ball, and pulls your arms, hands, and club through the ball. You want your left knee to get to the ball before the club gets to the ball. The knee kick is a bit quicker than it was on your chip shot because you're hitting the ball a greater distance. Your left heel may be coming slightly off the ground as your knee kicks in. Your ball jumps off the clubface with ease.

Instead of just slapping your arms at the ball (which is what most people do), you're now driving your lower body through the shot. You may never hit a fat one again. In *The Venturi Analysis*, Ken Venturi says, "leg action is the key to successful pitching." My own students' pitching improves 100% as soon as they start moving their left leg. The length of your backswing, the speed of your knee kick, and the length of your follow through are all factors that control the length of the shot. They change from one golfer to the next. Keying in on hitting an invisible tee under the ball will also help you hit down. Trying to swing up and hit the ball high only makes you top it most the time. You want to hit down, and your left knee kick helps you do so.

Your pitch shot will feel like two 'handshakes'. You shake hands on the backswing, which gets you into a good position. Then, hitting the tee, shake hands on the downswing. You'll end up on your left toe, (just like in the full swing) and your body will be facing

Photo 66: "Shake hands" on the backswing.

Photo 67: "Shake hands" on the follow through.

the target. Your body doesn't move as much or as fast as it does on a full swing, but make sure it does, in fact, move. *Photos 66* and *67,* on the fol-

lowing page, show the pitching stroke.

One extra note. On both your chips and pitches, your legs stay still on your backswing. Don't sway back or knock your "wall" over. Having your weight forward and your stance open at address usually eliminates any chance of this happening.

Pitching out of deep rough requires a touch and confidence that only comes with hours of practice. To have a complete knowledge of different lies, and how the ball will react, you should spend a bit of your practice time hitting out of bad lies. There are basically two different ways to hit out of deep rough, and these will be covered in the chapter on the playing lesson.

The Punch Shot

Learning to "punch" a golf ball may well be the smartest thing you'll ever do in this game. It's a shot that may be more helpful to you than any other, and can be mastered easily within a short time. I affectionately call it, "the best shot in golf."

A punch shot is a low running shot that you hit with your 5 iron. The ball stays low to the ground like a chip shot, and then rolls onto the green or fairway. You use your 5 iron to keep the ball low and eliminate any possibility of the ball popping up in the air too much, or from the clubhead going right under the ball.

I wouldn't recommend a 3 or 4 iron too often because the ball may not get airborne at all, and you might smother it. The punch is really just a big chip with one major difference. You don't land the ball on the green or in your Hula-Hoop. You roll it onto the green. Sometimes I call it the "British Shot" because it is one of the most played shots in Great Britain, especially during the British Open. The golf courses over there have hard fairways and greens, and lofting the ball up in the air and hoping it stops on the green is tricky.

The Address Position

When punching a golf ball, assume the same set-up as you just learned for the pitch shot. With your weight forward, stance open, and ball toward your left foot, you are in the correct position to hit this low runner. As in pitching, having your weight forward encourages a downward blow, and playing the ball back in your stance all but guarantees you'll hit the ball cleanly.

The Stroke

The punch shot feels very much like a big chip shot, except you give it a little more power. Keeping the wrists firm throughout, swing back to your handshake position. From here, the key element is your left knee kick. As you did on your pitch shot, kick your left knee in to start your downswing. The speed you do this will vary depending on how far you need to hit the ball, but be certain you do move it. Your left heel comes up off the ground slightly and you end up with the club pointing at the target. The ball will fly low; some 20% of the way, then roll the other 80%. It may take you a little bit of time to know how much backswing and knee kick you'll need, but you will notice that all your shots are rolling straight at the target. There's very little danger of hitting this shot off-line since your wrists are staying firm and your swing isn't too long.

Instead of having to gauge how high your ball will fly, and how far it will roll when it hits the green, you now only need to be concerned with your aim.

The average player will have much better success with this shot because it eliminates the need to get the ball airborne. It takes a precise stroke to slip the clubface perfectly under the ball when you're pitching, and if you're off by a fraction of an inch, a poor shot results. The punch simply rolls like a putt and stays low to the ground as it leaves the clubface. Even if you're a bit thin or fat, the ball still manages to end up on the green. It may not be pretty, but it's sure effective.

Where to Use the Punch Shot

1. Front of the green. If you find yourself in front of the green with nothing to go over, punch the ball and run it up close to the hole. You can do this anywhere from 10 to 100 yards away. Always ask yourself, "Do I need to go up?" If you don't, then punch it.

2. Out of the woods. If your drive ends up in the woods, take your 5 iron and punch it out into the fairway. Many golfers pick up their wedge and end up fluffing under the ball or hitting a branch. Keep it low and roll it down the fairway.

3. Hard pan. If your ball is sitting on hardpan or an old divot, hitting a lofted club is next to impossible. There's no cushion of grass under the ball and you may skull it. Sandy lies, pine straw, and loose soil are also times that the punch shot can be used.

4. In the wind. Lofting a sand wedge high into the air is only going to result in your ball being blown off-line too much. The wind won't affect your

ball if it's running across the ground.

5. Crowned greens. A crowned green is like an upside-down bowl. Trying to land a wedge on the green and make it stop will be next to impossible. Run the ball up onto the green for better control.

6. When you're nervous. Asking yourself to hit a high, perfect wedge to win the match usually results in disaster. If you're feeling a little shaky, knock it down and watch it end up close to the hole.

Some golf historians say golf was meant to be played on the ground and the punch shot is evidence of this. Just remember, if there's no reason to go up, then don't.

Sand Bunkers

For years, we've all heard golf professionals say that the bunker shot is the easiest shot in golf. Watching the pros on TV hit their ball out of a bunker and close to the hole seems to back this up. For most of us however, the sand shot wreaks havoc and creates fear when we have to play one. The bunker shot is difficult if you don't know how to execute it. But we're going to take care of that.

The reason a bunker shot is called easy is because it's the only shot in golf that you don't have to hit the ball. You hit the sand. Your club enters into the sand behind the ball, and you have an area about the size of a pancake to aim for. A pillow of sand carries the ball out without your club ever touching it. This pancake gives you quite a margin for error and being able to consistently hit it isn't too difficult. Your confidence and touch will improve the more you work on it. When was the last time you went to the range and practiced your sand shots?

Two Methods

I consider Ken Venturi the guru when it comes to the short game. His tips on the short game have helped millions of golfers, and whenever he talked, I listened. Venturi does sand a bit differently than most others, and I took what I learned from him and put it into practice with my own students. I also added some of my own ideas.

The traditional method taught for more than a hundred years is highly popular with most golf professionals, but in my own lessons I've found that most average golfers can't quite execute it consistently. I'll spend only a short time on the traditional way, because much of it will sound familiar to you, then concentrate on what I think you should learn and practice.

The Traditional Stance

1. Open your stance 45 degrees.
2. Open your clubface 45 degrees. You need an open clubface to counteract your body aiming so open.
3. Position the ball forward in your stance, and set most of your weight on the front foot.
4. Aim 2-4 inches behind the ball.

The Stroke

1. Cock your wrists up sharply on the backswing, taking the club outside the target line.
2. Hit 2-4 inches behind the ball steeply and explode the shot out onto the green.

Ok, let's talk about this. Nearly every article you read on bunkers tells you to do exactly this. Although it does work for some people (like pros with lots of talent and time to practice), I think it's too hard for the average player. First of all, why aim your feet way off to the right. Who came up with this? Most students will hit their shot off the right side of the green. Then, to stop this, they tell you to aim your clubface wide open. Do you aim your club like this on any other shot? Why not aim your body and clubface square, like you do on all your other shots? It makes sense to me to aim your club at the hole if that's where you're trying to hit the ball.

Here's why this method was developed a hundred years ago, and the mistake I think the golf industry made as golf went into the 20th century.

Gene Sarazen invented the sand wedge in the early 1930's. A sand wedge has bounce, as we discussed. The bounce enables the club to slide through the sand instead of digging into it. You should be quite clear on bounce by now, and how it has helped your chipping and pitching. Before the early 1930's, golfers could only try to hit out of the sand with a 9 iron or pitching wedge. These clubs dug into the sand because that's what they are designed to do. Well, I'm sure some old pro a hundred years ago tried to figure out how to stop this digging, and eventually stumbled on opening the clubface. Turning the blade open pulled the leading edge of the club off the ground slightly and kept it from digging. After hitting a few shots off to the left, our old pro decided he needed to aim his body to the right to get the ball going straight. Bingo! That's how this method was introduced to the golfing world and it's been taken for Gospel ever since.

I think that the year Sarazen invented bounce, someone should have said, "Hey, we don't need to stand like this anymore." Unfortunately, no one ever did. No one ever realized that with the invention of bounce, it was no longer necessary to lay the blade wide open, and in turn, there was no reason to aim the body open to the target line. The golf club itself changed dramatically. Shouldn't the original method that was invented to hit bunker shots be changed too?

Cocking and uncocking the wrists is also no longer as important as it used to be before bounce came along. Yet golfers, from coast to coast, are still picking that club up like they're chopping wood. When a pitching wedge was used to hit out, the ball must have gone over the greens quite often, so uncocking the wrists violently to try to create extra spin was a necessity.

A Better Method

I used to dread teaching a student bunker play because most of them only became frustrated with their lack of success. Now, it's one of the lessons I look forward to the most. In 10 minutes my students are popping the ball out onto the green nearly every time, and their reactions are normally one of utter contentment. After struggling for years, they now look like the pros on the Tour.

When the lesson first begins, I ask them to describe what they know, and how they rate their bunker play on a scale of 1 to 10. Nearly every one of them describes some of the traditional method, and their personal ratings are often a 1. After giving them the story of bounce, we begin.

The Stance

1. Stand only 10 degrees open. The reason you open up at all is to get your right leg out of your way during your swing.

2. Stand very wide. Your feet should be wider than your shoulders. With a wide stance you won't slip during your swing, your legs will be solid, and you are also lowering your center of gravity. With your feet too close together, your body feels too high.

3. Put 75% of your weight on your right foot. Setting the weight forward helps you hit into the sand.

4. Choke up a few inches. It's less than a full shot so you don't need the full length of the club. Since you've choked up some, the end of the club is sticking out of your hands. This is why you open your stance 10 degrees.

5. Set your clubface square to the hole. Unlike most other methods that have you open the blade, aim it at the hole. That is, after all, where you're trying to hit the ball.

6. Position the ball off your right foot. The ball will be in roughly the same place you would play your driver. Having the ball forward eliminates much of the possibility of your club hitting the ball before it hits the sand.

7. Picture a line drawn in the sand an inch and a half behind the ball. This is where you'll look, and where you'll line up your club to. Remember, you hit the sand, not the ball, so don't line your club up against the ball. Also, don't look at the ball. Look at the spot in the sand. To practice, you can actually draw a line in the sand. Hitting only an inch and a half behind the ball also lets you get the ball out cleaner and easier.

8. Have your shaft straight up and down at address. You don't want your hands too far ahead of the ball because it will take away the bounce on the bottom of your club. *Photo 68* shows the correct setup.

The Stroke

1. Take the club back to waist high with little or no wrist cock. That's right, little or no wrist cock. You're getting into your 'handshake' position again. This will be easy for you to do, because it's the same handshake position you get into in your full swing. Make sure you turn your shoulders and get your right shoulder behind the ball. It's easy to slip into the habit of only swinging back with your arms and leaving your shoulders out of it, so make sure you turn. Your arms and club are not heavy enough to power through the sand but your body is.

2. Keep your weight on the right leg, and maintain your wall and flex. Quite often I see students swing back and start straightening their left leg again. When this happens, your body

Photo 68: Set up for sand shot.

will rise up slightly and will cause you to miss the sand and skull the ball over the green. As we've said before, when you hit a ball thin, it's not picking your head up, it is standing up on the backswing.

3. Hit the "line" and follow through up on your left toe slightly. You must get off your left leg just like you do in your full swing. Far too often golfers stay flat-footed on their left foot and hit way too far behind the ball. Your weight starts out on your right leg, and gets more on your right leg as you follow through. The number one reason for hitting too much sand is staying too long on your left leg.

Your swing out of the sand is exactly like your pitch shot swing, and is very similar to your handshake drill on your full swing. You shake hands back to about waist high, and then shake hands on the downswing, ending up on your left toe. Your zipper may not have turned as much as on a full shot, but it does point near the pin. When you first start trying this, I think you'll notice that some of your balls may be short, and some may be long, but all of them are straight and most of them are out. Your number one goal is to get out in one shot. Even if you're not on the green for a while, at least you're out and didn't entirely waste a shot. As you get a little better, your goal should be to end up on the green, and eventually to get near the hole. Tour pros are trying to make their bunker shots and do hole them quite often.

The most difficulty my students have is their ability to hit the "line." It may take you a dozen swings to actually hit it and execute the shot correctly. This is simply your hand/eye coordination, and giving your body time to adjust to learning something new. If you hit too far behind the line, the sand will slow down your club too much and you'll leave the ball short. If you don't hit enough sand, your club will be moving too fast as it strikes the ball cleanly and will send it over the green.

With a little practice, your ability to hit the line will quickly improve, and you'll be on the road to success. You can actually practice your sand game without using golf balls. Go wherever you have some sand, even if it's in your back yard, draw a line in the sand, and practice hitting it. The line is what you hit during an actual shot, so hitting it a thousand times during practice will do you a lot of good when you get out on the golf course.

Controlling Distance

The ability to hit a bunker shot the distance you want comes through hours of experimentation on the range. We all have some feel when it comes to distance. We know approximately how hard to hit a 5-foot putt. Even novice golfers can roll their ball close to the hole, and usually don't knock it over the green. This internal feeling of touch is something we are born with, and it develops the more we practice a particular motion. There is no one there to tell you how hard to swing.

There are, however, several techniques that you can use to control your distance, either in the sand or on the putting green. Knowing what they are can expedite your learning. When it comes to bunker shots, there has historically been three ways to control how far you hit your shots. What you do to hit a short one, or a long one, has been controlled by one of these methods. All three methods do work, but in my own teaching, I use a different method that I think is easier to execute and just makes more sense. Venturi used to talk about this style and after seeing the success with my own students, I recommend you try it as well.

The Three Traditional Methods.

1. Change the length of your backswing. Many golfers take a short backswing to hit a short bunker shot, and take a long backswing to hit a long one. While this sounds logical, you have to change your swing from one shot to the next. Since I always want you to take the same swing to help your consistency, I don't use this method.

2. Swing slowly to hit it short, and swing fast to hit it long. Once again this sounds logical but you are going to have to change your swing. It's much easier to swing the same way every time.

3. Hit a lot of sand to hit it short, or hit very little sand to hit it long. No one is that accurate. I think it's hard enough just to hit the same spot every time. Always hit the same spot and you'll get good at hitting that spot.

The New, Improved Version.

I think it is better to change the length of your follow through. Granted, this is changing your swing, but it's not changing it until after the ball is gone. Take a short follow through to hit the ball a short distance, and take a long follow through to hit the ball long. I'll be the first to admit that if you measured my clubhead speed on the short one, I was swinging slower, but I didn't think slower. I thought shorter. My clubhead speed

was faster when I have a big follow through. Again, I don't think faster, I think longer.

The short follow through feels like checking your swing in baseball. Your club may come only to waist high on your follow through and your ball will fly a short distance. The long follow through is exactly like the follow through when you hit a full shot. The club comes all the way around you. You still want to hit your line as your follow through changes, and remember to come up off your left heel, even on the short one. This method allows you to swing the same way, with the same height, the same speed and the same line as your target. You simply change your follow through. Within a short time, your distance control will be much better and your ability to hit the ball where you want will be much improved. Other golfers may use one of the other methods with great success, but keep in mind that is only because they have practiced for years and have grooved their touch in doing so. I always like to do what seems most practical, and changing the follow through length gets my vote every time.

The Plugged Lie

If there's one shot in this game that makes grown men cry (and grown ladies weep) it's the plugged lie in a bunker. Affectionately known as the "fried egg," most golfers have no idea what to do when they encounter this little beauty. After two or three swings, and several pounds of sand, the ball is still sitting there as we see our good round disappear before our very eyes. Well, dear students, you no longer need fear this shot, and the technique you'll use to hit it is only one little change away.

Line up the same as you would for a normal bunker shot, as you have just read, but have your line in the middle of your stance instead of the line being off your right heel. The ball will still be one and a half inches in front of the line. By moving your line back some in your stance, your club will naturally come down a little steeper. Your ball is deeper in the sand, so you need to hit deeper in the sand. You don't have to change your swing at all. The simple act of moving the line back does everything for you. Picture how a pendulum swings. It starts out high, moves down until it flattens out in the middle, then gradually swings up high again. You're going to catch the sand while your club is still coming down. Instead of changing your swing or opening or closing your clubhead, this is all you need to do to get your plugs out. The ball will come out lower and will have little or no backspin. The ball will usually land on the green, but roll over since there's no backspin to make it stop. Since the ball is deeper in the sand, and you hit deeper in the sand, too much sand gets between your clubface and the ball, so there's no traction.

Getting close to the hole is not going to be your priority when your ball is plugged. Getting out in one shot is. There isn't much chance of a plugged shot ending up near the hole, unless the hole is way on the back of the green. In this case, the plug may actually help you as your ball will roll all the way to the back of the green and get close. It's very difficult to hit a plugged bunker shot to a close pin, and just as difficult to explode an unplugged bunker shot 100 feet or more.

Save your last ten balls in your range bucket for some sand shots. With just a little bit of effort on your part, the methods I have just outlined will have you looking like a pro in no time. You may even enjoy your time "on the beach."

Your short game is the key to lower scores. Whether it's chipping, pitching, putting, or sand play, your short game must always be sharp. There are too many moving parts in a full swing for it to work every time and hit the ball exactly where you want. As long as you can get the ball somewhere near the green, a solid short game can come to your rescue time and time again.

Chapter Nine:
Refining Your Short Game

Chapter Nine: Refining Your Short Game

The last chapter gave you the fundamentals of a solid short game. Once you've had some time to work on everything, you should see your scores start to drop in no time. The next step to your success comes from some of the intricate details you need to start thinking about. These small subtle items can be just as important to the over all picture.

The Spot.

A great putting stroke will make little difference if you don't aim your putt correctly. Reading the break, or seeing which way your ball will roll, is truly an art, and must be understood fully if you are to achieve success on the greens. The longer you play, the better you get, but you must know what to work on to shorten your road to success.

We've seen the pros on TV crouch behind their putts and stare at the hole. Here is what they are doing.

Crouching down a few feet behind your ball lets you get your eyes more to ground level and lets you detect the slope of the green itself. Obviously, if the ground to the left of the hole is higher than to the right, the ball will curve to the right as it nears the hole. How much it's going to curve is a skill that you can only learn through practice.

We're all smart enough to realize that the ball will curve down the hill, in this case from left to right, but there are some important details that must be addressed.

Let's say you have a 30-foot putt. You've crouched down behind the ball and have decided that the ball will break two feet from left to right. You should aim your clubhead to the spot that is two feet left of the hole and position your feet parallel to the spot. I think most of us do this. But then, right before we start our stroke, we take one last glance toward the target. But most golfers look at the hole. This is wrong! You should look at the spot. If you look at the hole, your brain will say, "I guess he wants me to start the ball at the hole since that is where he's looking." We end up either two feet (or more) off, or somewhere in between. Go for the spot, not the hole.

You often hear the announcers on TV say that every putt is a straight putt. They're absolutely correct! You're trying to putt the ball to a certain spot. Just the slope in the green curves the ball. You ruin any chance of starting the ball correctly if you look at the hole. The only time you should actually look at the hole is if you have a straight putt, which is quite rare. There is usually some break, even if it's an inch. If your putt was only going to break an inch from left to right, you should line up and look an inch left of the hole. You should also follow through at the spot, not at the hole. In the previous chapter you learned to point the club toward the hole. In putting, you should be pointing the club toward the spot.

This little detail makes a huge difference in your ability to start the ball rolling on line and make more putts, and is similar to another detail that you should do in your chipping game. Remember the concept of the Hula-Hoop. After choosing from your 5-7-9 or SW, your attention goes to your hoop. You know that the hoop should be two steps onto the green but make sure it's on line with where you want your ball to start. If you have a 50-foot chip that's going to break 10 feet from left to right, make sure your hoop is in line with a spot that's 10 feet left of the hole. Your hoop isn't in line with the hole. It is in line with your aiming position. The hoop should be in line with the hole only if your chip is going to be straight. Most professionals crouch behind their chip shots and read the greens like they do with their putts. If you were to position your hoop straight in line with the hole on a 10-foot breaking shot, your ball would end up 10 feet below the hole and you would never get it close. Take the time to assess the curve of the green and position your hoop in the proper position.

The High Side and the Low Side

A common phrase you hear every day on the golf course is the "high side and the low side." Let's go back to our 30-foot putt with the 2-foot break for a moment. After reading the green, you've decided that your putt is going to curve two feet from left to right. Anything to the left side of the hole is the "high side." It's the high side because that part of the green is higher than the hole. Anything right of the hole will be the low side. As your ball rolls, it starts curving toward the hole. It's breaking down the hill from left to right. As it slows down, if it's still left or high of the hole, it has a chance to go in. It looks as though it may stay a little left, but as the ball slows downs it may just drop in the hole on its last rotation. You made it. If, *On the Other Hand*, your ball is approaching the

hole and it's already beneath the hole, it's never going to go in. There is no way the ball will suddenly curve up the hill. From the moment you struck the ball it was already too low. You must give it a chance by playing enough break. If you don't make your putt, at least try to finish with the ball

Photo 69: Putt to the high side of the hole.

on the high side of the hole. You'll be surprised how many do fall in over time. See *Photo 69*.

Short or Long

Never up, never in! How many times have we all heard that? It's the one piece of advice we can all agree on. If you leave your putt (or chip shot) short of the hole, it's never, ever going to go in. It can't possibly go in the hole if it doesn't get there. We all know this. However, I would say that most amateurs I have played with leave their putts short 90% of the time. It may be going right into the center of the hole, but it stops two inches short. This is extremely frustrating. You read it right, you hit it where you wanted, the ball broke how it was supposed to, but you leave it short. Do this ten times during your round, and you've just added 10 shots to your score. Watch golf on TV for an hour and you'll see that if Tiger doesn't make his putt, nine out of ten times his ball rolls just past the hole.

Just as important as getting the ball on the high side is getting to or past the hole. If it doesn't go in, at least get it there. You must give it a chance to go in. Now, while this advice is obvious, there are a few extra reasons for getting it there that might not be so apparent.

If you hit the ball hard enough to finish a foot or two past the hole, the ball has more forward momentum so it won't break as much. This makes all your putts roll straighter. Since the putt is now going to break less, it's easier to read it. Just bang it straight into the hole. This is especially helpful on a short putt of two or three feet. It's really scary to have to start the ball outside of the hole on a three-foot putt. You have so much doubt as to how much it's going to break that you usually don't hit it with much confidence. If you stroke the ball with a little more speed, it takes the break out and your stroke becomes a straight putt. Instead of just barely hitting the ball and hoping it breaks, give it some speed and it will roll straighter.

Once you get outside the 10-foot range, you'll have to gauge your speed a little better and not be as aggressive, but on those short ones go ahead and hit the back of the hole.

The opposite would be hitting your putt too easily. As we just said, leaving it short gives the ball no chance of going in, but it also makes the ball curve more. If the ball is rolling slower, every little break in the green is going to affect the roll of the ball. When the ball slows down, it's going to break a lot at the end and you'll miss the hole on the low side again.

Next time you're on the practice green, try playing more break than you are used to on your long putts. See if you can leave the ball on the high side. I think you'll be surprised to see how many of them drop in. On your short putts, try being more aggressive and take the break out. You may well be on your way to cutting those extra strokes off your game.

The last reason for getting your putt slightly past the hole is determining the break. If you hit the ball a little too hard, and it rolls past the hole two or three feet, watch it as it does. You will see the break. When you set up to hit the little putt coming back, you'll know what to do. If you've hit your putt too hard and you know you're going to miss, don't turn away in disgust or you'll miss a golden opportunity to see the break. Watch your putt until it's done rolling and you'll learn how to hit it when you come back. Watch your partners. If you've seen the first three people hit their putts, you'll have a great read on how the putt is going to break. You'll have no doubt about where to aim since you've just seen it three times.

Uphill and Downhill

Putting up or down a slope can further complicate matters unless you realize a few things. Having a good enough eye to read the break can be of little reward if you don't consider the elevation change.

When putting uphill your ball will obviously need to be hit harder to get up the slope. Since you're hitting the ball harder, the break will be reduced. A 10-inch break on a level putt may only break 7 inches on an uphill putt. It breaks less because you hit it harder. You must be aware of this. Putting downhill is the opposite, and requires you to hit the ball easier to keep it from rolling too far past the hole. Since you hit it easier and the ball will be rolling slower, it will break more. That 10-inch break on the level putt may break 13 inches going down hill. Be careful.

Watching the Masters each April on TV is such a clear example of this. Augusta National has some of the fastest greens in the world. You see some putts that break 50 feet and look like they're rolling 1 mile an hour. The ball just goes and goes and goes. The ball curves more because it was hit extremely easily. Sometimes, even the best players in the world end up putting the ball off the green. Imagine what the 30 handicapper would do.

The green must be analyzed effectively before you can have a complete mastery of the short game. A properly executed putt or chip will never find the hole if the slope, speed, and grain of the green aren't examined.

Chipping and Pitching from Hard Pan

Hitting a golf ball off a tight or bare lie can be one of the scariest shots in golf. You don't have a nice cushion of grass holding the ball up, so getting the clubhead under the ball becomes more difficult. There isn't the margin of error available to you that the cushion of grass usually offers. When the ball is "sitting down," you must make a few adjustments to your regular routine.

The first: use a pitching wedge. Although the chapter on chipping and pitching advised you to become best friends with your sand wedge, you're now facing a shot that is out of the ordinary. The sand wedge, with its wide sole and bounce, will skull the ball over the green. The hardpan makes it impossible to get the bounce of the sand wedge under the ball. There's nothing to get under. The hard and bare ground doesn't give the way grass does and your clubhead will rebound up off the ground and hit the ball somewhere nearer its equator. The pitching wedge has "dig" like all the other irons do. The leading edge of the clubhead slopes down lower than the trailing edge and is designed to dig into the ground more. The pitching wedge can tear into the hardpan like a knife through butter and get under the golf ball. You'll still hit your Hula-Hoop like you did with your sand wedge. Remember that your pitching wedge is really just a 10 iron. Expect the ball to roll a bit farther since the pitching wedge has less loft than the sandwedge.

Play the shot with little or no wrist cock, a short backswing, and an aggressive left knee kick in toward the ball. Really concentrate on hitting down and following through. If you pretend the ball is sitting on a tee, it will help you to hit down better. The good news is you rarely have a tight or bare lie so close to the green. Usually the ten-yard area that surrounds most greens has nice full grass that is well maintained and is easy to hit from.

When pitching off a tight lie, the pitching wedge will again be the club of choice. When you're faced with a 30 or 40-yard pitch, and your ball is sitting down, the only way to get under the ball and hit a high soft shot is to get under the ground. Again, the sharp leading edge of your pitching wedge can cut through the hard ground and get the ball airborne. The shot is quite

Photo 70: To hit it out of heavy rough, the ball should be 2 inches outside of the player's left toe.

difficult and takes some confidence, but swinging down firmly into the invisible tee should be your mental image and result in a good shot. Remember that the 5 iron punch shot may work in this situation. As long as you don't have to go up and over anything, or the grass around the green isn't too long, the punch shot is far easier to play and execute.

Chipping and Pitching from Long Rough

Playing short shots from heavy rough is also no fun task. Knowing how the clubhead will get through the rough and where the ball will end up is anyone's guess. With a small change or two though, you can make this shot less difficult.

If you're in the chipping zone (less than 10 yards from the green) and your ball is sitting in deep rough, you must know two things. First, this will always be a sand wedge or lob wedge. These clubs are heavier. That makes it easier to get through the thick grass and the bounce on the club will slip through the grass better. A club without bounce, like the pitching wedge, will cut into the heavy grass and stop dead cold.

The second item is one that I give credit to Ken Venturi for inventing. He is simply a master around the greens.

When your ball is sitting in really long rough, play the ball about two inches outside your left foot. The ball is entirely outside the left leg, or is way back in your stance. (See *Photo 70*.) With the ball back so far, the angle your clubhead comes into the ball is as steep as it can get. This will get the clubhead on the ball without much interference from the grass. The club simply hits the ball before any grass has come into play. Be very firm with your wrists and really kick your left knee through the shot. The ball will come out quite nicely and will roll a bit after hitting the green. The Hula-Hoop concept doesn't really apply here because you're hitting the ball harder than you normally would. Even if the flagstick is toward the back of the green where you would normally chip with your 5 or 7 iron, stick with the sand or lob wedge. The 5 or 7 iron can't get through the heavy grass, and, playing the ball back so far in your stance is taking loft off the clubface. Your 5 iron would probably have the loft of a 1 iron with the ball in this position and would never get the ball out. Even the high degree of loft on your sand wedge has been lessened a great deal due to the backward placement of the ball. I'd say the sand wedge would have about the loft of about an 8 iron if you measured it. It is because of this that your sand wedge is your only choice. It may be nearly impossible to get the ball near the hole from this lie if the hole and flagstick are close to you, but that's OK. Your number one job is to get out. When the hole is cut on the far side of the green this shot is actually quite easy. You should be able to get the ball within 10 feet quite readily.

The pitch from heavy rough does require a more forward ball position. Take your normal pitching set-up but move the ball forward in your stance so it's an inch or two from your right heel. Open your stance about 25 degrees and open your clubface a bit. Set about 75% of your weight on your right leg. Swing the same as a normal pitch but with a bit more speed. The sand wedge will get though the long grass and will loft the ball onto the green. The reason you open the clubface is to give the club more bounce than normal so it doesn't get stuck in the heavy grass. You open your stance to counter act the clubface being open. After the ball lands on the green you can expect some roll because the ball doesn't have much backspin. The heavy long grass got between the clubface and the ball, producing what we call a 'flier', or a shot with little spin. Advanced players can land the ball a few yards short of the green and play for the bounce and roll, but this takes many hours to perfect. Keep your hands even or slightly ahead of the ball at address.

By adjusting your set-up and ball position you can see that many different shots are possible without having to change your swing too much. That's always made sense to me. Why change your swing when you only need to stand differently? After all, we spend hours on the range grooving our swings to perfection, why change or expect to change that swing at a moment's notice. Adjust your set-up, not your swing.

Chapter Ten:
The Playing Lesson, Part One

Chapter 10: The Playing Lesson, Part One

It's one thing to be able to hit the golf ball well and another to "play the game." Stepping onto the first tee requires not just a sound golf swing. It takes a strong mental strategy to make your way around the golf course in the fewest possible shots and with the least amount of errors. Venturi said, "The longest walk in the world is from the practice tee to the first tee." Learning to play the game requires imagination, patience, and an ability to process information that changes from one moment to the next.

I've never gotten too angry with myself for putting a bad swing on the ball. The golf swing is a complicated series of movements. What drives me crazy is when I make the wrong decision, pick the wrong club, or don't pay attention to the wind. While it may seem like there are a million things you need to think about before you even step up to the ball, don't panic. The following suggestions and thoughts are intended to help you SCORE. This is where course strategy and game management come in. They must be as big a part of your game as a proper grip. Without them, you're in for a long day.

Where to Tee the Ball

You arrive at the first tee, say hello to your playing partners, get your ball, tee, and club and walk up to the tee box. What do most of us do next? We tee the ball anywhere that's behind the tee marker and looks level, then swing away. About 90% of all amateurs choose to tee the ball in the wrong place. Your first important step in creating a successful shot is where you tee the ball.

Look down the fairway and analyze the hole. Try to see where the trouble is. Are there trees and bunkers down the entire right side? Is there water or out of bounds on the left? What you are trying to do is see where the trouble is. Choose a spot that you absolutely don't want to hit your ball toward. Then, tee the ball near the trouble side and hit away from it. If your first hole has trouble down the right side and the left is open, tee the ball on the right side of the tee box. From this position you will hit the ball away from the trouble side. It doesn't matter if you fade or draw the ball. Always do this. This gives you the best angle for your shot.

Let's do a bit of quick (and logical) analysis. Say you usually draw the ball from left to right. If you tee the ball on the right side and aim toward the left center of the fairway, and hit it straight, you'll be fine. If your draw works, you'll be even better. If you slice the ball, you'll also be fine since there's no trouble on the left. Even if you pull or hook the ball, because you've started the ball toward the left, you'll still be in good shape. You've given the ball the whole width of the fairway to hook and still end up in the short grass. Think of a tennis pro rushing the net. He has a better angle and his opponent can't get the ball past him.

If you had teed your ball on the left and aimed straight down the middle, any pull or hook at all is going to land you in the trouble on the right. You've basically cut the width of the fairway in half if you do this. Even if your normal shot is a fade, get over on the trouble side. Aiming to the left center will still find your ball in the fairway or at worst, in the left rough. Remember, we said there's no trouble down the left side. Even if you get a hook, your ball will find the fairway because you started the ball far enough to the left, so the hook only curves the ball back a little to the right. I've seen Fred Couples stand outside the tee markers with his feet to get the best angle, which is legal by the way, as long as the ball is between the markers.

Some Tour professionals may bend this rule a little because they are so good at shaping their shots. They know that they will always hit the ball a certain way and play for their particular shot. Most amateurs can't depend 100% on hitting the shot they're trying to hit. My advice is to stick to the rule. That way, from the moment you start, you're giving yourself an advantage over the hole. Remember, you are playing now, not practicing.

This rule does not apply on par 3's. In fact you do the opposite. On par threes your goal is to hit the green in one stroke. Let's look at a 150-yard par 3. If there's a bunker on the left front of the green, tee up on the right side of the tee box so you don't have to hit over the bunker. You don't want to force yourself to have to carry the bunker. In case you hit the ball a little fat or thin, or don't take enough club, the bunker would come into play if you teed on the wrong side.

Tee up on the side of the tee box that gives you a clear, open approach to the green, or away from any bunker or over-hanging tree limb. This way, if you do end up short, your ball won't be in the bunker. You may be short of the

green, but you'll only be left with an easy chip. Again, Tour pros might do the opposite from time to time, but they're good enough to hit the perfect shot time and time again.

Take a second to look at the layout of the hole before you put the tee in the ground.

Firing at the Pin

With apologies to amateurs everywhere, please just aim for the middle of the green. Most golfers are not consistent enough to aim at the flagstick. They look at the pin sheet for 5 minutes, take 6 practice swings, and then top the ball fifty yards down the fairway. Worse yet, they fire at a flag that's cut on the left side of the green, then push the ball ten yards more left and end up in the trees. Unless you're a single digit handicap, just aim for the middle of the green. This affords you the widest target, and allows the ball to be slightly off line and still hit the green.

The same goes for shooting at a pin that's cut behind a bunker. If you try it and hit the ball anything less than perfectly, you'll probably end up in the sand. Aiming for the middle of the green takes pressure off of you to hit that career shot and puts you in an easy two-putt range. You might even make the putt for a birdie. Basically, play within your means and play smart. Just because Ernie Els goes for the pin doesn't mean you should.

One last word on your approach shots. Select a club that will get the ball there, even if you hit it less than flawlessly. Again, being amateurs, we hit left and right, thin and fat. If your 7 iron goes 150 yards when you hit it like they do on TV and you choose the

7 when you're 150 out, you're forcing yourself to hit it perfectly. If you hit it almost perfectly, you'll be short. Choose your 6 iron when you're at 150 yards. In case you hit the ball a little fat it will still get to the green. It takes the pressure off. Also with the longer club you can swing a bit easier, which is always more easily controlled and executed. Amateurs are almost always short of the green and rarely go long. Think about your last round. How many times were you chipping back to the green? If you do hit the perfect 6 iron and you fly the green, you can congratulate yourself on hitting the ball too well.

Side Hill Lies

Quite often, we are faced with a shot with the ball on the side of a hill. This can be a bit tricky, especially since we all learn to hit the ball off a level lie on the driving range. Most golfers aren't very good off these side hill lies simply because they never have the opportunity to practice them. It's hard enough to become consistent in this game when the ball is sitting perfectly level or on a tee. Throw in the extra element of a hill and most of us are lost.

There are a few pointers that you need to know to take the fear out of side hill lies. Once you understand them, your game will become much more enjoyable.

Ball Above Your Feet

When the ball is above your feet, it has a strong tendency to curve to the right.(See *Photo 70A*.) With your feet below the ball, your swing becomes more of an "around you" stroke, like a baseball swing. This type of swing, as

Photo 70A: Ball above your feet.

well as how the clubhead sits on the ground, produces a hooking shot. Because the clubhead is well above you, the way the clubhead sits, or the lie angle, makes it difficult to start the ball straight like you could off a level lie. If you have a hard time remembering which way the ball will curve think of this. If you rolled the ball on the hill toward the target, which way would the ball go? It would follow the slope of the hill down and curve down toward the right.

Now that you know your ball is going to curve right, your next job is to figure out how much. I've always used the following as a guide. A 10-degree slope will move the ball 10 yards. A 20-degree slope will move the ball 20 yards and so forth. Let it curve. Don't try to fight the curve to the right, just know that it will. You simply have to aim the correct distance to the left. If I wanted to hit the middle of the green and I was hitting off a 20-degree slope, I'd have to set up and aim 20 yards to the left. Sometimes this actually requires you to aim off the green. Just take your normal swing. The slope of the hill will move the ball for you. It takes a while to trust it but it will happen.

The second thing you need to know is to choke down on the club. If the ball is 2 inches above your feet, choke down 2 inches. If you don't, you'll stub the clubhead into the ground too much.

Finally, when you choke down on the club, the shaft will not be as long as it usually is. This shorter club will shorten the arc of your swing and the ball will not go as far. Because of this, I recommend taking an extra club. Use a 6 iron instead of a 7. It will go about as far as your 7 iron. Off a very severe slope, you may need to take two or three extra clubs to make up for choking down. Your swing will be the same, as off a level lie. Just adjusting your stance, alignment and club selection will bring you success.

Ball Below Your Feet

When the ball is below your feet, everything is opposite. The ball tends to curve off to your left, and you'll need to make your club longer. Grip all the way up to the top of your grip so the club is as long as it can be. Since the ball is lower than your feet, you need to get down to it. Aim your body and clubface to the right somewhat to allow for the left curve of the ball. The same 10-degree rule applies. You may also want to take one club more to make up for the lost distance that a slice brings. A slicing ball never goes as far as a straight one, so you may want to use the 6 instead of the 7. Another reason for taking the extra

Photo 70B: Ball below your feet.

club is so you can swing easier.

Standing above the ball, balance becomes an issue. You are leaning forward so much, it's difficult to keep your balance with a hard swing. The extra club will allow you to swing more smoothly and easily, which helps you keep your balance. Finally, really stick your rear end out. You will need your backside to serve as your counter balance more than it normally does. Because the hill is trying to throw you forward, and your upper body is leaning over more than it usually does, you'll need a better counter weight. Exaggerate this more than you think you need to.

Uphill and Downhill

After mastering the side hill lies, you now need to know about hitting from a straight uphill or straight downhill.

Uphill

Hitting your ball from an uphill slope makes the ball go higher than normal. The loft of your 7 iron, for example, turns into the loft of an 8 or 9 because of the hill. The clubhead and shaft lay back, which increases the loft. Apply the same 10-degree rule. A 10-degree hill will require one extra club, and a 20-degree hill two extra. If you needed a 7 iron the hit the ball 150 yards, but you were on a 20-degree hill, you'll need a 5 iron to hit the ball the same distance.

The uphill shot will produce a pull to the right, much like the side hill lie that had the ball above your feet. The side hill is more of a hooking shot, while the uphill is more of a pull. This happens because you can't get your lower body (zipper) through the ball as well as you can off a level lie. The hill keeps too much weight over your left leg. It's nearly impossible to finish up on your left toe when you're hitting off a severe uphill slope. Since your legs move less, your arms and club come down too much and too soon, and they pass your body. This results in a pull. You're staying flat-footed and your arms are doing too much. Let the ball pull, just aim off to the left. A 10-degree hill will be a 10-yard pull, and a 20-degree slope will be a 20-yard pull. I've hit off some slopes so severe that I needed to aim 60 yards to the left. It's hard to make yourself aim so far off line, but you have to.

Every once in a while, something else may happen. Because you stayed flat-footed, and your legs and zipper never got through, the clubface comes through wide open and you actually slice the ball. Your arms never rolled over like they should because the lower body didn't get out of the way. The clubface stays open and you hit the ball 50 yards out of bounds to the left. It's a rarity but it does happen. Concentrate on maintaining your normal swing to avoid this.

Downhill

A downhill slope will produce a low push, the direct opposite of the uphill. The ball goes lower because the slope de-lofts the clubhead. For example, a 7 iron turns into a 5 and the ball goes much farther than you expect, because it flies so low. Use the 10-degree rule again to take a higher lofted club. A Tour pro could hit his 8 iron 200 yards off a severe down slope since the 8 iron is playing like a 4 iron. It's good for your ego but that's about all.

The ball will push to the left because your body gets out in front of the ball and clubhead too much on the downswing. The slope is pulling your body toward the target, and you almost walk through the shot. The clubhead has a hard time catching up and stays open through contact, resulting in the push or slice. That 10-degree downhill slope can all but guarantee your ball going 10 yards to the left. Aim to the right and let it push.

On both the uphill and downhill shots, make your body conform to the slope. In other words, lean with the slope. If the hill is going up at a 20-degree angle, make your knees, hips and shoulders slope the same way. Do the same for downhill. This way, your body is working with the slope and you won't stick the clubhead in the ground. Don't stand into the hill, stand with the hill.

For all these tricky lies it wouldn't

be a bad idea when you're on the range to go off the side or back of the hitting area and find some hills. Spending time getting used to uneven shots can certainly benefit you in the long run. The same advice would go for hitting some practice shots out of the rough or off the hardpan. You don't always have a perfect lie when you play 18 holes, so you must practice off of less than perfect, flat lies. No one hits all the fairways or greens and your ball can certainly come to rest in some ugly places. If you've figured out what to do with shots like this before you actually encounter them, you'll certainly have a better understanding of what to expect. Sometimes when I walk up to the range with a basket of balls, I'll throw them up in the air, a few handfuls at a time, and hit them from wherever they land. Some are in the rough, some end up in old divots and some are lying nicely. Regardless of where they sit, I hit them, and closely watch how the ball reacts and flies through the air. The next time I play, when I have one of these weird shots, I'm not so quick to panic. I've hit the shot many times on the range and can step up to the shot with a good deal of confidence.

Wind

My father and I were out on a very windy day a few years ago. As another of his perfect approach shots got slapped into a greenside bunker for about the fifth time in the round, he turned to me he and asked, "How can it be that every shot is into the wind? I haven't had one down wind all day." The wind can be like that.

Playing on a windy day can frustrate you beyond belief. You fire a perfect shot right at the pin only to have the wind blow it into the bunker. You did everything right but you end up in poor position. Wind has a noticeable and tremendous influence on your golf ball. Realizing that your ball only weighs a little over an ounce, it's not hard to see that a 30-mile an hour wind will move your ball all over the golf course. They don't even launch the Space Shuttle on a windy day. Learning how to play in the wind is a part of the game we all need to understand, and applying a few common sense techniques will save you hours of frustration.

Into the Wind

We all tend to swing harder when the wind is blowing at us. We try harder, tense up, and usually don't pull off a very good shot. The wind intimidated us into doing something we shouldn't have. Don't change your swing. Change your strategy.

You will be 10 yards shorter when you hit into a 10-mph headwind. That translates into 1 club. Hit your 6 instead of your 7 and swing the same. The ball will go the 7-iron distance. A 20-mph wind is a "two club wind." The other reason the lower lofted club will be better is that the ball will fly a bit lower and not be affected as much. You're staying "under the wind." A club with more loft makes the ball balloon up too high and the wind really grabs it. If you think you will hit too far with the longer club, choke up one half inch on the grip. Making that 6 iron a little shorter, decreases the normal arc of the swing and the ball will fly like you've hit it with a 6 1/2 iron. Also, when you choke up, the shaft becomes a little stiffer, which makes you hit the ball a bit lower and shorter.

A regular flex shaft becomes a stiff when you choke down on it an inch or so. Keep your swing the same. Make all the adjustment before you even step up to the ball. Playing into the wind requires a smoother swing, which of course requires a longer club. Hitting the ball a bit easier also puts less spin on the ball, which keeps it from ballooning up in the air. If you try to hit your normal club (the 7 iron in this case) harder, not only will your swing get too jerky, but the ball will come off with more spin and rise up too high. An aircraft carrier turns into the wind when preparing to launch its planes. The wind gets and holds the plane up in the air better than on a calm day, just like it will do to your golf ball.

With the Wind

With the wind at your back, the ball will travel farther than normal. The 10-mph tailwind requires you to hit one less club, your 8 instead of your 7. The ball also flies lower because the wind is knocking it down, so the 8 iron will make up for your lost height. Stopping the ball on the green is also harder for the same reason. The wind wants to push the ball over the green. Taking the 8 will naturally produce more spin. We all hit better when the wind is behind us because we're not trying to hit the ball any harder. We tend to swing easier, which usually produces a better shot. An advanced player may land the ball on the front of the green because he knows the ball will not stop as fast as it normally would.

Left to Right Wind

Lefthanders love this wind. Your slice will certainly slice less if the wind is blowing left to right. Your straight shot will have a slight draw. It's only bad if you have a natural draw because the left to right crosswind tends to overdraw your ball. However, most of us wouldn't be too unhappy curving the ball to the right a little more. Aim your set up about 10 yards to the left for a 10-mph cross wind, and 20 yards left for a 20-mph cross wind. The wind simply blows the ball back straight. The mistake I see many amateurs make is trying to hold the ball into the wind, or trying to curve the ball against it. Let the wind be your friend and work with it.

A Tour professional may have the ability to curve the ball the opposite direction the wind is blowing, but for most of us this is asking for trouble. Trying to curve the ball into the wind greatly reduces how far it flies and you come up short. If you ride the wind, hitting the ball far enough will never be a problem

.

Right to Left Wind

You're in trouble if you have a slice. The spinning motion of the ball, which produces the slice, is significantly amplified in this wind. Your ball will slice more because the wind is not only pushing it to the left, but is adding to the spin. Setting up a bit to the right and taking your normal swing is the smart thing to do. Your ball will get up in the wind and blow off to the left. You have to play your slice and adjust for the power of the wind on that particular day.

You could also close your clubface slightly. This "hooding" of the clubface delofts the club somewhat. This keeps the ball under the wind more and counteracts the effects of the right to left crosswind. Before you try this, work on it on the range. You may close the clubface too much and hit a viscous hook if you're not careful. Again, let the wind be your friend and don't try to fight it.

Gauging the Wind

Here are some tried and true tips that will help you figure out how the wind will influence your ball flight.

A) Toss grass up in the air. We all know this one. Look where the grass goes and that's your wind.

B) Look at the flagstick. If you don't feel any wind on your face, look how the flag is blowing.

C) Look at the tops of the trees. This is better than just looking at the flagstick. Keep in mind your ball doesn't fly flagstick high, it flies tree high. Also, the green and flagstick may be sitting in an area that is protected from the wind.

D) Look at the waves on the water. If you're hitting over a pond, see which direction the ripples are going. This is a great one.

E) Look at the birds on the ground. They always face toward the wind, ready for takeoff. They are much like our aircraft carrier.

Fairway Bunkers

I always get a kick out of showing a student how to hit out of fairway bunkers. They think the lesson is going to be extensive and it will take me an hour to show them. I tell them that you hit out of a fairway bunker the same as you hit from the fairway, end of lesson. The two shots are almost identical. There's nothing I do from the fairway bunker that I don't do striking

a normal shot from the grass. Well, almost nothing.

First, take one more club than you normally would, a 6 instead of a 7 for example. You cannot (and shouldn't) swing as hard from the sand. You'll slip. The sand doesn't provide as solid of a foundation as the grass does. The extra club helps you be a bit smoother and still achieve the required distance.

Second, play the ball in the middle of your stance. If the ball is too far forward, toward your right heel, you run the risk of hitting the sand before the ball and you may hit it fat. You can still play your 8 through wedge back where they belong, just don't ever position the ball ahead of center. Also, don't try to hit too much club with too little loft. Trying to hit a 3 iron or wood out of a fairway bunker is just asking for trouble. I don't even attempt anything lower lofted than a 5 iron. Maybe a 7 wood, or 9 wood, but be careful. You don't want to leave yourself in the bunker.

After choosing the proper club and positioning the ball correctly, simply swing like you normally do when on the grass. Your goal is a little slower tempo and staying steady. What makes these shots so hard is the margin of error. If you're afraid of digging into the sand too much and strike the ball a little too high up, you'll hit it thin or top it out of the bunker. Hit a little behind the ball and you get too much sand, causing the ball to be well short. Think of hitting a particular spot on the ball. Swinging with a little slower tempo will help you be more precise. You still want to finish up on your left toe like in a normal swing, and keep your legs steady during the backswing (the wall).

Most of us aren't very good from the fairway bunkers because most driving ranges don't have fairway bunkers. It's kind of hard to be good at something if you never have the opportunity to practice them. Maybe on a late summer day you can go out by yourself when there's no one else around and try a few from the fairway bunker. It's really the only way you're going to have the confidence when faced with this shot, and confidence is 90% of it. If you had a bunker on the range you'd quickly see that this shot really isn't that difficult once you try it a few times.

One more thing Venturi taught me. Never try to slice the ball out of a fairway bunker. Many amateurs assume they're supposed to because that's what they were taught to do from a greenside bunker. Coming into the ball with the clubface open too much will give the ball a weak glancing blow that will only end up short and left of your target. The sand gives way (unlike the firmer grass) and the ball is never pinched and compressed enough to go anywhere. What you want to do (physically as well as mentally) is try and draw the ball out of a fairway bunker. Contacting the ball with a slightly closed clubface makes impact easier and cleaner, and of course produces a nice draw that goes farther. Even if you just think of hooking the ball out of the fairway bunker you'll get better results. The "hook feeling swing" is also a flatter, more around your body swing, as if you were hitting the shot with the ball above your feet. Your clubhead's approach into the ball will be more shallow. This reduces digging into the sand too much, and you avoid the fat shot.

To sum up, take one extra club, play the ball more in the center of your stance, use a three-quarter swing, and feel like you're going to play a draw. If I had to add one more item to your menu, it would be to put a little more weight on your right leg at address. The extra weight on the right leg helps get you off your left side better, and increases your chances of a clean hit.

112

Chapter Eleven:
The Playing Lesson,
Part Two

Chapter 11. The Playing Lesson, Part Two

Strategy

Playing a round of golf is very similar to playing a game of chess. You're always looking ahead, planning your next move. Where do you want to be? This is not to say that you should be thinking three holes ahead, or not be fully concentrating on the shot at hand. What this does mean is having the mental capacity to analyze the shot at hand and assess the risks and rewards. Should you fire at the pin or is it too dangerous? Should you lay up or go for the green? Should you cut the corner or play safe down the middle?

These are all examples of questions you should ask yourself before making your play. Where will your ball end up if you don't pull off the shot you're trying to hit? Just in case you don't make it over the trees on the corner, what kind of trouble could you get into? That's what I mean about thinking ahead. We're all fascinated when Tiger Woods pulls off one of his miracle shots. But remember, in addition to being maybe the greatest player in history, he's practiced these shots before. He'll go out on the course after hours and create the most impossible set of circumstances for himself and try and recover. He's not attempting a shot he isn't moderately sure he can actually hit. For most of us, playing safe and smart is the best way.

Let's say you have a short par 4, about 290 yards. Many Tour pros could easily drive the green. Maybe you could too. But is it smart? Are you actually going to drive your ball 290 yards dead straight? You know you did it once on the range about 10 years ago, but think about it. What is the more likely scenario? When you try to hit it that hard and long where do you usually end up? Trees? Lake? Bunker? Fifty yards to your left?

On a 290-yard hole, you don't need a driver. Even if you teed off with a 4 or 5 iron you'll only be left with a short wedge into the green. Your chances of hitting it close are quite high. You may even make your birdie putt. At worst, you'll two-putt for your par. Do that 18 times and you'll be a happy camper. Think about scoring, not muscle.

A 450-yard par 4 requires a big tee shot. The only way you'll hit the green in two is if your tee shot puts you in good position. These holes are often called "demanding." An appropriate description. Having to hit the ball long and straight is putting quite a burden on your swing. But if you break the hole down into sections, everything becomes possible.

I think a great way to decide on what club to hit from the tee box, especially on that long 450 yard par 4, or when playing a new course for the first time, is the "150 marker rule." Most of us can hit the green, or somewhere near it, when we're 150 yards away or closer. This distance is usually a 6,7 or 8 iron. These clubs are easier to hit. Well, if you're faced with a 450-yard par 4, simply subtract the 150. You probably can't smack it 300 yards with confidence. But you can probably hit a 180-yard tee shot. Your second shot will put you well within the marker. From there you hit the green and go for par. There's never anything wrong with par and the pressure is off.

What about a 330-yard hole? You want to get to or past the 150-yard marker. We are at 180 yards again. For this tee shot you'll probably only need an iron. A 210-yard tee shot would only leave you a wedge into the green. You simply don't need a 300 yard tee shot on a 330-yard hole. Play it smart and safe. The iron off the tee will certainly find the fairway more often than the driver will. The single digit handicapper or Tour pro may hit a driver because they have a higher rate of consistency than the high handicapper does. Just because you've done it once on the range, don't count on it happening on the golf course. The better and more you play increases your consistency and lets you gamble on the long clubs ... a little more. For now, just score.

The same holds true for par 5s. You may not need a driver off the tee just because it's a long hole. The opposite may be true. Unlike the Tour pros, most amateurs cannot hit a par 5 in two shots. Reaching a par 5 in two shouldn't even an issue. If you're not going to hit the green in two, why bother with a driver? In other words, even if you hit your best drive, let's say 260 yards, you'll still be left with a second shot of nearly 300 yards. Most par 5's are over 500 yards in length, so a 260-yard drive will still leave you over 240. Not many of us can hit a second shot of 240. Since you're never going to get on in two, why bother with a driver that you may hit sideways.

I tell low handicappers this story. Faced with a really long par 5, let's say 590 yards, the low handicapper gets up on the tee and thinks, "Wow, I'm really going to have to crunch this one."

This is backwards thinking. Even if this golfer hits a 300-yard drive, he'll still be left with 290, and there's no way in ... *well you know* ... that he'll hit his second onto the green.

If this golfer was on a short par 5 of 460 yards, then a big drive would be advantageous to getting on in two. There's a possibility of reaching the green in two with a big drive on this hole, but virtually no chance on the big, long par 5. People really think backwards in these situations. When you're faced with a long par 5 why not hit a 3 wood or long iron off the tee. From there, since hitting the green is out of the question, another mid to long iron will get to the 100-yard marker. A wedge shot later, you're lining up your birdie putt. Three easy iron shots will get you in birdie range nearly every time.

Trying to hit the green in two with a driver and 3 wood is just asking for trouble. Not only are these clubs harder to hit, but you will also probably swing harder than normal because you're trying to reach the green in two. With a swing like that, the percentages of your flubbing the shot increase dramatically.

I can't tell you how many times I'll speak with a golfer that recently played in an "irons only" tournament at his club. On this fun event, the golfers are required to leave their woods in the bag and only use their irons. I'd bet that more often than not the golfers shoot a lower score than they do when they use their woods. They may not hit the ball quite as far but they also rarely get in any trouble. Down the middle, then on the green, without the fear of hitting the ball into trouble. It's certainly easier to hit the ball 190 yards straight than it is to hit the ball 300 yards straight.

Play smart, play safe, think what you're doing, and your scores will drop dramatically, I guarantee it!

Out of the Trees

We all occasionally find ourselves in the trees during our round of 18 holes. While the trees provide shade and a source of beauty, finding your ball behind one can be most frustrating. Your number one job when you're in the trees is to get out. Even if you can't hit the green (or see it), get out of the trees so you can hit your next shot. Far too often a golfer will hit his tee shot into the trees then stay there for his next three shots. Trying to hit the miracle escape shot only gets him into worse trouble than he was to begin with.

A great story comes to mind about Raymond Floyd. Floyd found himself in the trees after his drive and the gallery quickly surrounded his ball to watch his next shot. As he was sizing up his shot one of the gallery members said, "Ray, why don't you start the ball out low, then curve it around to the left and make it rise over those two trees and roll it onto the green." Floyd answered, "If I was that good I wouldn't be here to begin with!"

We all find the trees from time to time, and knowing what the smart play is can save you some shots.

First, think low. Your best bet is to use a 5 iron and punch the ball out into the fairway. The 5 iron will get the ball out and send it rolling down the short green stuff with consistency. Trying to hit a lofted club like a wedge is just asking for trouble. First of all, slipping the clubhead precisely under the ball is

demanding (you may hit it thin or fat), and trying to gauge how high your ball will fly is anyone's guess. Why bother hitting it up in the air when that's where all the branches are. Run the ball low with the punch shot. Even if you hit the shot a bit thin or fat it will still get out of the trouble. Put yourself in a position to hit your next shot from the fairway, where chances are you'll find the green.

Staying in the trees is never going to work very well. Being in the trees should cost you one half of a shot. What this means is if you were in the trees ten times, five of the times it will cost you a bogey, while the other five times you'll be able to scramble and save your par. The golfer that tries for the heroic shot usually ends up making a double or triple bogey, which instantly ruins your round. You can bounce back from a bogey by making a birdie somewhere, but coming back from a triple is devastating. You're so angry at making the triple that the rest of your round is no good because you're so upset. If you hit your drive into the trees, then play a smart punch down the fairway, who knows, you may even hole your next shot for a birdie.

In Between Clubs

Sometimes you're faced with a yardage that's right in between two of your clubs, like a 6 and 7 iron. You feel the 6 will go too far, but also don't think the 7 will get the ball all the way there. What do you do? There are actually several choices you can make to hit this "tweener" right on the pin.

First, always take the longer club, in this case, the 6 iron. You never want to try and hit the 7 harder for reasons

116

I've mentioned. Taking the 6 iron allows you to be more relaxed and swing easier, which will always produce a better shot. There are just a few adjustments you need to make to hit the 6 the correct distance.

Choke down a little. Choking down even an inch makes the shaft shorter, which reduces the arc of your swing, turning your 6 into a 6 1/2. Choking down also stiffens the shaft.

The other method, little known to most golfers, involves your left leg. Take your regular address position. Now, step two inches back (away from the target) with your left leg. This stepping back motion rocks the arms and club back slightly, which adds loft to the clubface. You're laying the club back slightly and turning your 6 into a 6 and a half iron. You don't open the clubface. You lay it back. With the same swing the ball will fly the distance of a 6 and a half iron. Instead of changing your swing, or swinging easier, you're simply stepping back two inches and adding loft the club. It will take you a few shots on the range to figure out how much to move, but it's really a neat way to hit the ball different distances with the same club.

Intentionally Curving the Ball

While we all strive to hit the golf ball straight, there are times when you need to "work the ball," or hit a shot that curves one way or another. Having the ability to curve the ball at will can only add to you having a complete game and mastery of the golf course. As with the half shots, wind shots, or hill shots, knowing a few simple things can complete your resume as a shot maker.

To hit a shot that intentionally curves from left to right (a hook), making a few adjustments in your setup and stance is all you'll need.

First, strengthen your grip. Instead of the 'V's of your grip pointing up at your left ear or up your left arm, make

Photo 71: Intentionally curving the ball.

them point outside your arm. By turning both of your hands a bit more to the left, the 'V's will now point a few inches outside your left arm. In this position your hands become too strong which will cause them to be over active on the downswing. (See *Photo 71*.) The hands will roll over too much, which will cause the clubface to close. The closed clubface will hook the ball to the right. How much you strengthen your grip will dictate how much the ball will hook. With the same swing, the ball will hook because the hands did too much. It may take your brain a while to figure out what you're doing and swing the same, but it will happen.

The other method is to close your clubface slightly at address and leave the grip alone. You're swinging and gripping the same, you're only closing the clubface before you swing. This will result in a shot that starts off straight for a few yards then curves violently to the right. This is good if you need a severe hook, like around a grove of trees.

If you want to the ball to fly left to right with not as much of a curve, you'll need to do something a little different. Close the clubface slightly at address, but aim your feet a bit to the left. Your body is left of the target and your clubface is right of the target. With a normal swing, the ball will take off to the left, then slightly curve to the right with more control than the "snap hook." With your club, swing and path, you should try to start the ball where your feet are aiming and shouldn't swing down the line where the clubface is pointing. This may confuse your body for a while, but learn to trust it.

To hit the ball right to left (a slice), do the opposite.

Move your hands to the right some on your grip. This is a weak grip, which will keep the clubface open through contact. The open clubface will cut across the ball imparting slice spin on the ball. Align your feet and stance a little to the right to make the ball start slightly right. Your key tip is this: Aim your feet where you want the ball to start, and aim your clubface where you want the ball to finish.

Your club will swing down your body line, then curve the ball back to where the clubface was pointing. Let me give you an example.

You want to hit a 180-yard shot, but there's a tree directly in front of you. If the tree is too high to go over, you'll need to curve the ball around it. To slice it around the tree from right to left, you'll aim your feet and stance to the right of the tree, let's say some 20 yards. From here though, you'll aim your clubface at the middle of the green. With a regular swing, the ball will start off 20 yards to the right of

the tree, then curve back to the left. The initial blow to the ball starts the ball right of the tree since your body was aligned there. As the ball flies, the slicing spin takes over and moves the ball to the left. In reality, your clubface was aimed square at the pin but was 20 degrees open to your body alignment. You're simply trying to hit a straight shot like always, but you had an open clubface, which imparted slice spin to the ball.

Your first few attempts may send the ball to the right as your brain is trying to correct this "wrong" looking position, and may close the clubface at some point in your swing. Your brain is thinking something doesn't look right here and makes an adjustment to help you hit the ball straight as you normally would. You must keep the clubface in this open position during the swing for the slice to work. It's hard but stick with it.

If you wanted to hook the ball left to right around the tree you would do the opposite. Aim the clubface at the middle of the green, but align your feet and stance to the left some 20 degrees. The clubface is looking straight at the pin but is actually closed to where you're aiming. The ball will start off to the left, then curve back to the right. Again, you have to swing down the alignment of your body and not open the clubface.

Some professionals can curve the ball by changing their swing some during their stroke, but this is too difficult for the average player to groove. If you are a five handicap or lower, here are some professional alternatives.

Some Tour pros, if they intentionally want to draw the ball, will actually **open** the clubface at address. With their clubface sitting open they know, consciously and sub-consciously, that they need to close it during the downswing for their draw to happen. Because they're talented golfers with supreme control of their swings, they can manipulate their arms, hands and clubface to close before impact. It's open at address, so they close it during the swing. They have little fear of over-hooking the ball since the clubface was open at their setup. Ben Hogan fashioned a swing similar to this. He opened the clubface drastically during his backswing, and then slammed it shut on the downswing. He felt he could hit very hard with his right arm and hand and still not be afraid of hooking the ball, since the face was wide open to begin with. He developed this swing to fight the snap hook that plagued him in the early part of his career. He felt that when he was under pressure, his right hand became too dominate and rolled over the left too much during the downswing, causing a severe hook. Through many years of trial and error on the range, he decided to roll the clubface open to stop the hook.

If the advanced player realizes his clubface is open at some point in his swing, he has enough talent to close it right before impact. The average player would slice the ball from this position because the clubface would stay open throughout the swing. It's interesting though, to be able to cure someone's slice by **opening** the clubface. You'd think the ball would slice more, but the advanced player knows he must close it up and usually does.

When the Tour pro wants to intentionally fade the ball, he sometimes sets up with a **closed** clubface. During the downswing he'll actually open the clubface by hanging on longer through impact. Instead of letting the wrists roll over, he keeps his hands a bit firmer through the shot, which keeps the clubface from rolling over. His thought is, "It's closed so I must open it." Players that grip the club with a strong grip do this as well. Gripping the club with a "hook grip" makes them swing through and hang on longer than is considered normal. The hanging on keeps the hands from rolling over too much and prevents the hook. Fred Couples and Paul Azinger are prime examples of this. They have very strong grips, which in most players would cause a hook, but they hang on through the impact zone longer than most players do and actually play a fade.

This whole opposite sounding theory does work, and does work quite well, but keep it on the back burner until you're shooting those par rounds.

Chapter Twelve:
Clubfitting

Chapter 12: Clubfitting

Getting a set of golf clubs to fit your body size, type and swing is a huge step on your road to a better golf game. Club fitting is the art and science of "fitting" a set of clubs to a particular individual. From my experience I would say that at least 90% of all golfers' clubs don't fit them properly. Most amateurs buy their clubs off the rack or order them out of a catalog. That would be like asking a thousand people to wear the same size shoes. The Tour players certainly don't buy their clubs off the rack. They may play the same brand of clubs that we do, but their clubs are matched up perfectly with their height, arm length, leg length, swing speed, strength, flexibility and hand size. Some golfers buy the latest "wonder" club, and spend $1,000 doing so, but they're throwing their money away if the club doesn't fit them. That's like spending $1,000 on a suit but not having it tailored to fit your body.

There are several important measurements that must be taken into account to properly fit a set of clubs to the golfer: lie angle, length, shaft flex, swing speed, hand size, flex point, set makeup and clubhead design. Once you understand these terms, they will help guide you when you select your next set of clubs. Of course, your first step should be to find a PGA Professional who is well trained in club fitting. He or she can clearly show you what to look for and why being fitted properly is so important.

Lie Angle
(Note: Check out the chart on Page 134 to see the dramatic difference the lie angle can make.)

Without a doubt, the most influential element in hitting a golf ball straight is the lie angle of your golf club. Without the proper lie, even the world's greatest golfer couldn't hit the ball straight.

Photo 72: As the shaft of the club gets closer to you, the lie angle lessens.

Think of a croquet mallet. The handle, or shaft, sticks into the mallet head straight up, forming a 90-degree angle with the top of the mallet. The lie angle for the mallet is, therefore 90 degrees. As that shaft gets closer to you, the lie angle lessens. (See *Photo 72.*) For example, a putter is close to having an 80-degree lie angle. A five iron has a lie angle of 60 degrees.

Most golf companies use the 60-degree lie angle on a five iron as the industry standard. If the lie is not right for the golfer, the clubhead may strike the ground with the toe or heel of the club higher than the rest of the club. Instead of the entire sole (bottom) of the club hitting the ground, only part of it does. So, if more of the toe of the club hits into the ground than it should, the toe digs in too much and opens the clubface. You'll always be fighting a slice. If the heel digs in too deeply, the grass grabs the clubhead and makes it close, causing a hook. The club has either a too "upright" or too "flat" lie angle.

During a club fitting session, your pro begins by placing a hard plastic "lie board" on the ground. Then, he'll place a special piece of tape (yes, it's called "lie tape") over the entire sole of your club. The tape has lines on it like the lines on a ruler. He places a ball on the board and has you hit some shots, banging the board as you swing. When your club strikes the board, it will leave a little mark on the tape. The goal is to have that mark in the direct center of the tape, which would be in the middle of the sole. That's what should happen. In most cases the mark is a bit toward the toe or heel. This

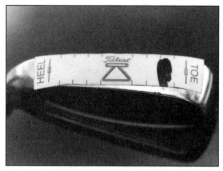

Photo 73A: A "flat" lie.

shows that the lie angle of your club is wrong, and the sole of your club is not striking the ground flush.

If the mark is toward the toe, this means that the lie of your clubs is too flat. (See *Photo 73A*.) The angle of the shaft going into the clubhead needs to be more acute, or more upright, toward vertical. Because the lie is too flat, and the toe of the club is digging in too deeply, the clubface opens at impact and you slice the ball. Even with a perfect swing, your golf ball

will slice off to the left. The lines on the piece of lie tape are measured in one quarter inch increments. Each line is exactly one lie degree. If the mark is one line off toward the toe, your clubs are one degree off. If they're two lines off, they're two degrees off and so on.

Now here's the really scary news. When you hit a five iron 170 yards, a lie angle just one degree off causes your shot to be three or four yards off line. Just one degree! Two degrees off will make it six to eight yards off line, even if you swing perfectly. Imagine how far off a 250-yard shot would be!

You may have clubs where the lie is too flat but you hit the ball straight. You might even hook it sometimes. What you've been forced to do is make adjustments and compensations to try and stop the slice from happening. Sometimes you won't adjust at all and you slice. Other times you'll adjust just enough and actually hit the ball straight. Or you'll adjust too much and hit a hook or pull. Well, "sometimes" is a lousy word. You want to hit it well all of the time.

Let's look at it this way. If your clubs are 2 degrees too flat, the ball will slice 8 yards. If you ever hit the ball straight, you've actually pulled it 8 yards. The pull in your swing stopped the slice in your clubhead. But this is not the way to play golf. Why not have a golf club that will hit the ball straight when you swing correctly. It's a lot easier to develop a sound, consistent golf swing if you don't have to change it every other time.

Now, let's go back to the lie board. If the mark consistently stays in the same spot (in this example 2 degrees toward the toe), you will need a club that is 2 degrees upright from standard. Instead of playing a 60-degree lie on your five iron, you need a 62-degree club. With the same swing, the mark on the piece of lie tape will now be dead center. We gave you a 2-degree upright club because yours was 2 degrees too flat.

If the mark on the lie tape is toward the heel of the golf club, your clubs are

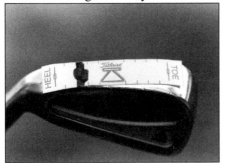

Photo 73B: A too"upright" lie.

too upright. (See *Photo 73B*) If your 60-degree lie angle is hitting too close to the heel (two degrees), you'll need a 58-degree club. Your pro will have an assortment of clubs in his fitting cart that has every conceivable lie angle imaginable. After establishing what you need, he'll pull out the correct club and let you try it. Almost instantly your shots will fly straight at the pin, or curve some to the right with a nice draw because now your clubhead is striking the ground properly. With the same swing you've always had, your shots are instantly better because your clubs are better!

Now let me make another point here. The first few times you try your new club, you may hit huge pulls or hooks to the right. That is because, over the years, you have grooved a pull swing to stop the slicing action your old clubs caused. You've mastered the pull because you've had to. You're the King of the Pulls at this

point. When you pick up a club that has the proper lie angle, the ball will no longer start off to the left. You swing and your pull happens, and off the ball goes to the right. You've always had that much pull but it's now just showing itself. A few minutes with your pro can bring your swing back to where it should be.

In my own experience as a club fitter, the average amount most clubs are off is six, even seven degrees. Remember, just one degree off results in a shot that is three or four yards off line. Imagine being 7 degrees off! Some golf professionals feel that the flex of the shaft is the most important element in your golf club, but there's no convincing me that it's not the lie angle.

The lie angle is measured by how far your arms hang down to the ground. The distance your fingertips are from the ground is important because that's where the club comes up from. It doesn't matter how tall you are (you don't hit the ball with your head), it matters how long your arms are. Taller people generally have longer arms, and shorter people generally have shorter arms. After the golfer has assumed the correct address position and his arms are hanging comfortably down, the club needs to lie in his hands properly, with the sole of the club resting on the ground. Occasionally during the lie board test a student will swing poorly and feel that the mark on the lie tape will be wrong. He says, "let me swing again and I'll hit this one better." In reality, how you swing from one effort to the next really doesn't matter. It's not the swing the dictates where the mark will be, it's the length of your arms, and that's not going to change.

A junior player may grow a few inches as he reaches adulthood, but most of us buying clubs have matured physically. A golfer with extra long arms usually needs flatter clubs because his arms hang down closer to the ground. A tall person with short arms usually needs a more upright lie so the grip reaches his hands more comfortably.

Length

After the pro has determined the lie angle of your clubs, he must next check the length. To measure this, he attaches a piece of tape to the face of your club. When the ball is struck, it leaves an imprint of the ball on the tape. The goal is to have this imprint in the direct center of the clubface, or sweet spot. A ball that is struck off center, toward the heel or toe, will fly much shorter than one hit in the sweet spot, as much as 20%. It has been documented through testing that a 170-yard five iron hit just a half inch toward the toe will only go 136 yards. That's not going to lead to many good rounds. The ability to consistently hit the sweet spot has a direct relation to your club's length.

The standard length throughout the golf industry on a five iron is 37 and 3/4 inches. This is where the club fitter begins. Your own club may be longer or shorter, but the 37 and 3/4 inch length is standard. After affixing the face tape to your club, the pro watches you hit a few shots, then checks where the imprint is. If the mark is consistently toward the toe of the club, your clubs may be too short. A longer club would move the mark toward the center. If the mark is too close to the heel,

the club may be too long. I say "may be" because your swing will influence where this mark is. The lie angle mark wouldn't move, but this one does.

You may produce a mark that is off center because your swing is less than perfect. The mark may be too close to the heel simply because you are standing too close to the ball at address. The mark may be toward the toe because you're too far away. The mark may be toward the toe because you swing down and come over the top, forcing your club to swing on an "out-to-in" path and hit the ball on the toe. There are hundreds of possible reasons the mark may not be in the center because the average player does something different from one swing to the next. The golfer that had a wrong lie angle on his clubs, then made an adjustment to compensate, may never hit the ball in the middle of the clubface regardless of how correct the length is.

A good club fitter realizes this and considers how the club looks in the golfer's hands at address. Does he look too bent over? Does he look uncomfortably straight? Is his weight toward his toes too much? Maybe the golfer is leaning over too much because his clubs are too short, or maybe the golfer is leaning over too much because he doesn't know the proper way to stand to begin with.

While I nearly always change the lie angle of my students' clubs, I rarely change the length too much, and never more than an inch. When you make a club longer, it becomes more difficult to hit. If the club is longer, it's harder to square up the clubface and hit the ball dead center. Granted, you'll hit the ball a little bit farther if the club is a little bit longer, but the loss of distance created by an off-center hit negates this small advantage. With a club that is one inch longer, you can hit the ball three or 4 yards farther. But hitting it one half inch off center results in a hit that is 20% shorter! The risk is too great.

An advanced player or Tour professional may be able to handle a longer club but most amateurs won't. My own personal feelings are the worst thing the golf industry has done to golf clubs in the last ten years is make them longer. A standard driver today is 45 inches long. The standard used to be 43 inches. I've seen some drivers that are 48 inches long! The golfer hits it farther, but farther into the trees. Tiger's driver is only 43 and a half inches long and he's certainly not a short hitter. Longer is only better if you can hit it square and straight.

Changing the length of the golf club does something else very important. It changes the lie. This is what we need to spend a little bit of time discussing.

Everyone has a friend at his or her club that does club repair. Your friend says, "You know I can make your clubs longer and you'll hit the ball longer." You excitedly take his advice and he lengthens your clubs. WRONG! He just messed up the lie angle. It's very important that you know this. Whenever you change the length of your club, you'll change the lie. Every half-inch you lengthen a club changes the lie angle by 1 degree. That 60 degree five iron you've been hitting will become 61 degrees if you lengthen your club a half inch. If you lengthened your five iron by two inches, (which would be ill advised) the lie would become 64 degrees or more

upright. You'll never hit the ball straight.

Let's say the lie angle that you hit your mark in the center of the sole on your five iron was 60 degrees. Let's also say that your club was standard length. Well, if the pro determines you need an inch longer club, he would now fit you to a club with a 58-degree lie. Combined with the extra length, the 58-degree lie will play like a 60-degree lie. This is called the "effective lie." It's what the lie plays to as the club is actually being swung. How the club sits in your hands is not how it will hit during the swing because of centrifugal force and other factors. You can't just change the length without changing the lie. An expert club fitter knows this and takes it into consideration during your club fitting session.

Shortening your clubs is fine and may lead to crisper ball striking but only to a point. Obviously a club that's too short is not going to achieve the required distance. Be reasonable in your length changes, with an inch either way being the accepted maximum. During your club fitting session, if the ball imprints are all over the face, the pro may suggest a lesson before the fitting session continues. This is an indication that your swing has some major flaws and that you never hit the ball the same way twice. It's difficult to determine what length is best for you if your swing is so inconsistent.

Once the ideal length has been established, and the effective lie angle has been determined, it's time to move onto your swing speed, which determines your shaft flex.

Shaft Flex

You may have heard this before: the shaft is the engine of your club. This is quite true. The only thing that connects you to the head of the golf club is the shaft. What shaft and flex you should be playing with must be determined with great accuracy before you order your new clubs. A general rule is that the faster you swing, the stiffer the shaft you'll need. If you have a slower swing, you need some extra flex.

A golfer with a slow swing needs some help in hitting the ball far down the fairway, and a shaft with a bit more kick to it will do just that. The "whippiness" in the shaft kicks in at the last moment to help you hit the ball a fit farther. A golfer with a powerful swing doesn't need as much help and instead, needs a shaft that's a bit firmer to control his accuracy. Anyone hitting a whippy shaft will indeed hit the ball farther, but loses a bit of control in the process. What shaft the individual needs is best determined using a swing speed machine.

The pro puts a small device down on the ground, about three feet behind your ball. It's the size of a small camera and measures your clubhead speed much like a radar gun. What speed you consistently produce tells the pro what flex you need. Tiger Woods swings his driver at nearly 130 mph, while the average player is in the 75 mph range. A quick look at these two numbers should tell you that these two guys shouldn't be using the same shaft. Tiger needs a very stiff shaft to match his powerful swing, while the other fellow should have some kick to help him hit the ball farther. An average woman golfer may be in the 60 mph range and require a really whippy shaft. In my years in golf I would say that far too many average players play a shaft that is too stiff for them. I think ego may have something to do with it, but you should be realistic. What I ask my own students is, "The Tour pros use stiff shafts. Are you a Tour pro?" I read a test a few years ago that said Jack Nicklaus used shafts that were closer to being 'regular' flex than 'stiff'. If Nicklaus used regular, should you be using stiff?

A more flexible shaft also allows you to hit the ball a bit higher, which is usually a good thing. As the shaft kicks in it will get your ball up in the air a bit easier and give you more distance. A very stiff shaft will produce a lower trajectory with not much hang time. The Tour pro may want this, but most of us would benefit from the added height. We all need help getting a long iron up in the air more, and a shaft with a bit more flex will do it for you.

A major golf equipment manufacturer does comprehensive testing on shafts and swing speeds and has a chart that clearly shows golfers which shaft they should be using. When I'm doing a club fitting myself, I rarely see swing speeds of more than 90 mph. If your pro doesn't have a swing speed machine, his years of experience should be able to determine what flex you need.

The kick point of the shaft should also be determined. *This is where the shaft flexes.* There are basically three different points for you and your pro to choose from.

A high kick point means the shaft is flexing up near your hands. This will produce a lower ball flight, as the tip end of the shaft is quite stiff. This is the choice of Tour professionals. They already hit the ball high enough and are frequently trying to keep the ball low and beneath the wind. They hit the ball with enough power to get it into the air. They don't need the shaft to get it too high.

A mid flex point is for many average to better than average players. This shaft doesn't hit it too high or too low. The shaft matches up with the player's ability and fits to many golfers that regularly shoot in the upper 70's to mid 80's.

A low flex point is for slow swingers that need some help getting the ball airborne. Seniors, ladies, juniors and high handicappers can benefit from this shaft. It is the one I put in at least half my own students' clubs.

A more flexible shaft also helps you draw the ball a bit more. As the club swings down and the shaft kicks in, the shaft is actually trying to close the clubface through impact. Because the shaft 'bows' a bit, the clubhead is closing up slightly as it approaches the ball. The more flex, the more it bows. This is a piece of information that 99% of golfers don't understand. Let me explain.

If there's one myth that I spend more time on than any other it is this. A very whippy shaft will actually 'hook' the ball to the right. Most golfers think just the opposite. A student will say, "I keep slicing my driver so I'm thinking about putting in a stiffer shaft." They think, and it's easy to see why they do so, that as their hands approach the impact position, the shaft is curved back with the clubhead lagging behind. They think that the clubhead isn't going to catch up

and that it will stay open as it strikes the ball. I must tell you, just the opposite is true.

High-speed pictures of a swing show that the clubhead does lag behind during the start of the downswing. But they also show that as the

Photo 74: The clubhead gets to the ball before your hands do.

hands near the ball and slow down some, the shaft bows forward and the clubhead actually gets to the ball before your hands do. (See *Photo 74*.) It happens with every golfer, with every shaft and with every club. The clubhead is getting to the ball before your hands are and has closed about 2 degrees. This helps the ball draw some. It has also been shown that a very stiff shaft will hit the ball low left. The golfer that has been hitting low slices is only going to compound his problem more by putting in a stiffer shaft.

The next step is the weight of your shaft. This one's easy. Lighter is better. There is absolutely no advantage in having a golf club that's just heavy. It will only slow your swing down. Now if you're a golfer that has tried everything to slow your swing down and you still can't, then a heavy shaft may do the trick for you, but I'd work on your swing first. If the shaft is too heavy, the club head won't have much feel. Putting a lighter shaft in your club, the clubhead will be easier to feel since the shaft is lighter. The weight of the club is distributed is better. You don't want the weight in the shaft; you want it in the clubhead since that is what hits the ball. This is called the swing weight, what the clubhead weighs in relation to what the entire club weighs. You want the overall weight of the club to be lighter so the clubhead will feel heavier. You want more mass down there actually hitting the ball, and less weight under your hands.

One final point about shafts. Where the shaft bows forward some on the downswing and closes the clubface slightly through impact, the shaft also bends in a direction that drops the toe of the club slightly. This is called "toe drop', and must be considered during your club fitting session. During the downswing, because of centrifugal force, the head of your club actually drops down a little with the toe getting lower than where it started at address. The evidence has shown that the toe drops about two degrees at impact. Think about it. At address, if the sole of your club is absolutely flat on the ground, it will return flatter, or with the toe of the club digging into the ground slightly. Because of this phenomenon, the toe of your club must be about two degrees off the ground during your address position. This is why you must actually hit balls when doing a club fitting and not just measure

from a static position. A driver may have more toe drop because it's longer and the shaft may flex more.

A more flexible shaft will have more toe drop than a stiffer shaft and your club fitter takes this into account. After you have determined the lie and length of your golf club, and selected the proper shaft, you must hit a few more shots to make sure everything is working in harmony. Putting in a more flexible shaft could actually flatten the lie of your club, while making the club longer can make it more upright. When these elements are working together, you will have that perfect set of clubs.

As you can see, the shaft is "the engine of your club" and must be right for you. What flex, flex point and material (steel or graphite) you need can only be determined through a club fitting session.

Grip Size and Style

What style grip you choose is strictly personal preference, as is how it feels in your hand. But getting the correct size must be measured accurately. There are a few simple guidelines to measure your hand size to fit you with the proper grip. Grip the club in your right hand only. You should have about one half inch sticking out of the back of your hand for control, and never be all the way down to the very end. Now look at your hand. Your middle two fingers should just be touching the fat, meaty part of your hand or the lower part of your right thumb. (See *Photo 75*, next page.) If these two fingers are pressing in too deeply, the grip is too small. If there is a gap between your finger and this pad of your hand, the grip is too big. Your

Photo 75: Your middle two fingers should just be touching the fat, meaty part of your hand or theμ lower part of your right thumb.

pro will have an assortment of different grip sizes for you to try out. They're measured in 32nds of an inch, but it's enough to make a difference. If you had to have too big or too small, always get the one that's too small. A grip that's too big will reduce the action of your hands during the swing and may produce an open clubface through impact, causing a slice.

Some grips are a bit heavier than others, which makes the head of the club have to be heavier to offset this. This causes the overall weight of the club to become heavier, so be careful in your selection.

Head Style- Irons

Even though there seems to be thousands of golf club manufacturers and tens of thousands of different types of clubs, there are really only two different head styles: a cavity back and a blade. Ninety-five per cent of clubs made today are of the cavity back variety and because of their design, are easier to hit. They're called cavity back because much of the

weight has been carved out from the back of the clubhead and distributed around the perimeter. Instead of the weight being directly behind the ball it's now around the edges of the club. This keeps the clubhead from twisting too much during impact and lets you hit more shots that stay straight. This perimeter weighting is much more forgiving when your ball and your clubhead's "sweet spot" don't quite meet. Ping golf company was the creator of this style of iron and most of the clubheads we see today are based on the Ping design. Different companies have different size cavities with various weight distributions. Fortunately, especially for left-handers, the selection of very good clubs has greatly improved.

The other style clubhead available is called a blade, which dominated clubhead design for as long as golf has been around. This clubhead is solid from heel to toe and has no cavity in the back. It produces a very solid feeling when the ball is struck correctly, but has a much more defined sweet spot. If the ball hits toward the toe of the club, even a little, the toe will kick open since there's no perimeter weighting to keep it straight. This club demands a dead center hit and is nowhere near as forgiving as the cavity back. Better players lean toward playing blade style clubs for several reasons, but feel and appearance determine their choice.

To many advanced players, a cavity back iron just looks too big. They prefer looking down on a more compact head and tend not to like anything that looks too oversized. You'll often hear this described as a "clean look." If a player has used a blade style club for many years, or has grown up playing them, they'll never like the look of any oversized club.

Average players usually think just the opposite. They like looking down at their club and seeing a slightly larger hitting area. The larger head gives them the confidence that they're going to hit the ball better. A high handicapper does not want a blade style club since the sweet spot is too small for them to find on a regular basis.

A question you may be asking is, "Why wouldn't every golfer, including the pros, want the biggest sweet spot they can get?"

The answer is a Tour pro wants to know and feel when he's hitting the ball slightly off the sweet spot. If his swing is a bit off and he's catching the ball slightly toward the toe of the club for example, he wants to realize he's doing it so he can correct his swing. With a cavity-backed golf club, a toe hit may feel just as good as one that's hit dead center. This player can't be sure if he hit the ball in the sweet spot or if it just felt like he hit the sweet spot. The pro knows that a slight toe hit now may lead to a bad toe hit in a few months if it goes unnoticed. He would prefer to go to the range and improve his swing rather than just "get away with it" for too long. On the other hand, the amateur player usually doesn't want to spend all his free time on the practice tee. He simply wants a club that hits the ball straighter and produces more good shots.

Unless you are a low handicapper, don't bother with the blade style clubs. They're simply too hard to hit well on a consistent basis. But I do hope that when you've applied what you've learned in this book, you will all be 2

handicappers and sales of blade clubs will skyrocket!

Set Make-up

It's now time to decide what and how many clubs you need to buy. A great benefit of custom club fitting is that you can order what you want and are not obligated to buy a whole set. You can always order another club later to fill in any gap you may find in your distances.

The USGA allows you to carry a maximum of 14 clubs in your bag. With the putter in there you're down to 13. So choosing your set composition is vitally important. What clubs you decide to order has much to do with your ability and swing speed. Ordering a one or two iron may not be the best choice for you if you're a slower swinger. While your professional will guide you toward what's best for you, I'll also give you some ideas.

For the irons I would start with a 5-SW. These are clubs that are not only important but are easy to hit. You may have a sand wedge that you really like but remember, if you keep your old one it's not going to match the rest of your new set. Go ahead and buy the new one. Do you need a three or four iron? Your answer will come from knowing what your clubhead speed is and how far you hit the ball. A slower swinger, under 70 mph, does not need these two clubs. There isn't enough loft to them to get the ball up in the air if your swing speed is this slow. A 5 wood would be a better choice. Because the head of a wood is bigger and rounder, and has a lower center of gravity than irons do, it is much easier to hit than long irons. The distance a five wood hits a golf ball is just about the same as a three or four iron. The difference is that the five wood is easier to hit and will get the ball airborne better. The five wood is also better out of the rough, since the rounded head will slip through the grass instead of digging into it, like an iron does.

A low handicapper with a higher swing speed probably should carry a three and four iron. This player is good enough to hit these low-lofted clubs and may like keeping the ball lower when hitting into the wind. A Tour professional likes a one or two iron for much the same reason. These irons can achieve the length they desire, but with better accuracy than woods. A one iron matches up closely with a three wood for distance, but the three wood goes higher. Just be smart and realistic when assessing your abilities when choosing long irons. Save that one iron until you're shooting par on a regular basis.

On the other end of the bag are the wedges. How many wedges you need and what style you should have are issues you need to again look at very closely. Most manufacturers now offer four wedges in a set. They include the pitching wedge, gap wedge, sand wedge and lob wedge. You'll need a pitching wedge in your set so there's no loft gap in your bag. The pitching wedge is the "ten" iron in your set and you really have to have one when you're too close to hit a full nine, say from 110 yards.

The sand wedge may be the most important club in your bag other than your putter for the reasons we have described in this book. You chip with it, pitch with it, and, of course, hit the ball out of the sand with it. It is a cru-

cial club in your bag and you must have one. A standard sand wedge has 56 degrees of loft. Use this as your starting point when thinking about your other wedges. There's no reason to order a 55-degree club if you already have a 56. You usually have a 4-degree difference in between clubs, so your pitching wedge will have 52 degrees.

All clubs made over ten years ago were set to these standards and it made knowing what to buy quite easy. Recently however, club companies have started making clubs with "stronger" lofts. Stronger means less loft. Today, a pitching wedge only has 48 degrees of loft and nine irons have 44. The companies do this for two reasons. First, they can claim that you'll hit their clubs farther. Obviously. Less loft equals more distance. But that new pitching wedge you're hitting isn't a pitching wedge at all. It's a nine iron! It says PW on the bottom, but it has the loft of an old nine iron. It's good for your ego but understand what's actually happening.

Not only can the companies claim longer shots, they've created a reason to buy another club. They call it the gap wedge. Unfortunately, for your pocketbook, you're going to need one. This club has the 52-degree loft that the old PW used to have and, in fact, does fill a gap between the new PW and the new SW.

With lofts of 48 and 56 degrees respectively, there's now an 8-degree gap in your set. You won't have a club to hit the ball this distance unless you buy the extra club. If a good player hits his 56-degree sand wedge 100 yards, his PW will probably hit the ball 130 yards. There's now a 30-yard gap with no club. Short of changing your swing some and inventing a shot, there's no club in your bag for the 115-yard shot. Thus, the gap wedge was created.

The last wedge is the lob wedge. These clubs have more loft than the sand wedge and have the same bounce as the sand wedge. The usual loft for these clubs is from 60 to 64 degrees. They were invented for hitting the ball over bunkers and trees, and from 30 to 50 yards. Actually, I think they're great!

Instead of changing your swing to hit a short shot with a 56-degree sand wedge, you can pick up a lob wedge and basically swing the same. Because of their tremendous lofts, lob wedges allow you to hit high, soft, short shots. The "partial" shot becomes easier because now you have a club that does it for you. I actually use the lob wedge for chipping, pitching and half shots, and can also hit it from 90 yards or so. I use my lob wedge far more often than my 56-degree sand wedge and I think you will too. In my opinion, I think it's the best invention the golf industry has come up with in recent years.

With four wedges in your bag, and the 9-5 irons and putter, you'll have room for four more clubs. Maybe you can add that four iron later, or put in a seven or nine wood to go with your driver, three and five. Do some experimenting and monitor your swing speed to determine what clubs are best for you.

The Driver

Without a doubt, an issue I spend as much time discussing with my students as any is: Should you use a driv-

er? The reasoning and rationale behind my explanation is quite in-depth and is as important as anything I discuss with my students regarding club fitting. I encourage you to read and reread this segment until you understand it thoroughly.

Many golfers tell me that they actually hit their 3 woods farther than their drivers. While this doesn't sound logical, they are absolutely correct in their assessment. The reasons why are a little technical but let me explain and tell you of a test that backs this up.

An independent test had the "Iron Byron" (a swing machine) hit a driver several times. In case you haven't seen it pictured, the "Iron Byron" is a strange looking machine that was designed to hit the ball perfectly with any club. The Iron Byron never miss-hits. The driver in this test had 9 degrees of loft, which is considered the industry standard. The clubhead speed was set to120 mph, or that of a long hitting Tour professional. When this 120-mph swing hit with this 9-degree driver, it produced a drive that went 300 yards. The Iron Byron hit the ball ten times in a row and consistently produced the same result.

Then, a special batch of golf balls was introduced that were smooth, with no dimples. The ball looked like a Ping-Pong ball on the outside, but was otherwise a standard golf ball.

With the same driver and clubhead speed the ball only went 100 yards! What this showed was that approximately two thirds of the flight and distance of a golf ball is in the spin, or aerodynamics. The dimples catch air as the ball spins and creates lift. The extra lift makes the ball stay in the air longer and you achieve more distance.

The 9 degrees of loft (which isn't very much) could only get enough spin to keep the ball airborne if it was hit very hard, like with a 120 mph swing. If the clubhead was only going 90 miles an hour (or three quarters as fast), it would put one quarter less spin on the ball. If the clubhead speed were only 60 mph, the ball would have only half the initial spin rate. With such a low spin rate, the ball would go out a hundred yards then fall to the ground. The 9 degrees of loft combined with the 60 mph swing simply didn't generate enough spin to keep the ball in the air. What this test showed us is that the slower you swing the more loft you need.

Now let's talk about a 3 wood for a minute. A standard 3 wood has from 15-17 degrees of loft or nearly double that of a 9-degree driver. Anyone hitting this club will put double the spin on the ball compared to a driver. The spin rate is nearly double because the loft is nearly double. What these numbers show us is that if your clubhead speed is less than a Tour pro, you're going to need more loft to achieve the same spin rate.

The PGA of America has said that the average clubhead speed for amateur men is 75 mph. 75. Some of you may be more or less, but this was the national average. According to my calculator, a 75-mph swing is 38% slower than the 120-mph swing of the Tour pro. Using this figure tells us that the average player requires a clubhead with at least 38% more loft to get the same spin rate. This would make the 9-degree driver into a 12-1/2 degree club. The 75-mph swing combined with the 12 1/2 degree loft will give you the same spin rate as the 120 mph

swing and 9-degree club. Got it? Since they don't make too many 12-1/2 degree three woods, get one that has the standard 15 degrees of loft.

Let's look at another type of golfer. Joe is 80 years old and has a clubhead speed of 55 mph. Joe is currently hitting a big headed driver with 8 degrees of loft. He says his favorite Tour pro drives one 320 yards and he just has to have the same club. The reality of the situation is that Joe is never going to hit this club anywhere near this distance with his swing speed. A 320-yard drive would require a swing speed of more than 120 mph. Joe's 55 mph swing is less than half of that and would require a club with at least 16 degrees of loft to work at all. Joe may even want a five wood with 20 or 21 degrees of loft to get the ball airborne. Along with the higher loft, the 5 wood has a smaller head and lower center of gravity to let him get the ball up in the air more easily. Joe should buy a five, seven and nine wood, and leave the long irons and driver in the bag (or even better, in the display rack).

Bottom line is, if your clubhead speed isn't 90 mph or higher, you don't need a driver in your bag. If you're at 80 to 90 mph, use the three wood. If you're less than 80 mph, you're better off using a five wood as your driver. Be honest when figuring out how fast you really are swinging. Find a pro who has a swing speed monitor. It can save you loads of frustration as well as a few dollars.

Finally let's talk about the accuracy factor. If a club has more loft and puts more backspin on the golf ball, it will decrease the amount of sidespin, which causes the ball to go left or right. The more the ball is spinning backwards, the less it's going to spin sideways. A 20-yard slice on a 9-degree driver may slice only 10 yards off a 16-degree 3 wood. Just try to slice your sand wedge and you'll see that you can't. The 56 degrees of loft puts so much backspin on the ball that any sidespin is negated. You might pull or push your wedge, but you'll rarely slice it. The 5 wood will slice less than the 3 wood for exactly the same reason. More loft, more backspin, less sidespin.

Apply this information practically and choose clubs with the right lofts for your game. The right size, set make-up, shaft and head style are all very important in getting the most for your golf game. Though it is tempting to believe some of the claims made in the advertisements, it is best to seek out a qualified PGA professional who can guide you through the vast assortment of clubs on the market. He or she is highly trained in this field and can make sure you select the proper equipment.

THE TRUTH ABOUT LIES...

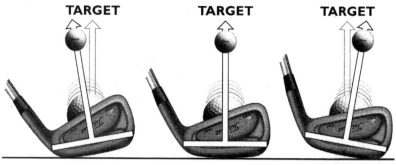

Lie Too Upright
(Ball left of target)

Correct Lie

Lie Too Flat
(Ball right of target)

Illustration courtesy of Titleist.

Chapter Thirteen:
Advanced Instruction
for Your Golf Swing

Chapter 13: Advanced Instruction for Your Golf Swing

At this stage, you should understand the fundamentals of a sound golf swing and short game, and may be experimenting with the different options I have made available to you. By options I mean trying out different swing thoughts and ideas to see which works best for you. An example could be the chapter on your "handshake."

You could think "handshake" or "triangle." You could think to turn your shoulder behind the ball or turn your right shoulder under your chin. You could also think, "turn 90 degrees." All of these different swing thoughts are doing the same thing. For your wall, you could think, left leg, right heel or "keep your knees flexed." I've simply given you a variety of ways to do the same thing. If you try them all out, one at a time, you'll no doubt find the one that works best for you. Five different people might like five different ideas. They're all basically doing the same thing, they're just thinking of different ways to achieve it. You may use one idea for a while with great success, then find that in a few months, another idea works better. There's no rhyme or reason why, except that golf is a very fleeting game and most ideas only stay with you for a short time. Bobby Jones was once asked what he thought about during his swing, and his answer was, "Whatever the last thing was that worked". Even at the highest level of professional golf, there never seems to be just one idea that always works.

It is with this concept in mind, that I offer you this chapter.

Throughout my 20 years of teaching I have had to expand my list of swing thoughts to accommodate the wide array of golf swings that I see on a daily basis. The longer I teach my list of ideas, explanations and analogies grow, as does my ability for spotting problems. Getting a student to understand a particular part of the swing can involve several different explanations until it finally sinks in. What follows in the next few pages are some of those different explanations that I usually use after I've worked with a student several times. I introduce the three fundamentals to every new student that I work with and give him sufficient time to learn and get comfortable with them. Through checkup lessons over a period of several months, I always make sure the big three are still there and that the student is performing them correctly. After some time passes, I usually start getting into a few new, and more advanced items that can take him to the next level. I always work off the three fundamentals (the handshake, the wall and the zipper) but start adding to his arsenal. A student has to first learn some portion of the swing before they can be shown others. With this in mind, and your 3 fundamentals looking good, let's start the new stuff.

The Advanced Handshake

As discussed in Chapter 3, the handshake is the most important move you can work on in your golf swing. Having a full shoulder turn on the backswing is the key to hitting the ball with any power and accuracy. Turning your shoulders 90 degrees and getting your right shoulder 3 or 4 inches behind the ball is your highest priority.

To this point you've been keying on the turn of the right shoulder and the position of the right hand as it reaches the handshake position. When a student has mastered this over several months on the range, I then introduce the idea of "pulling your left shoulder behind you" to start the backswing. Instead of thinking push and turn the right shoulder behind the ball, now think of pulling your left shoulder directly back behind you. You'll notice that your right shoulder does indeed turn behind the ball as your left shoulder pulls back, it's just a different feeling. It would feel like someone was facing you with his hands on your shoulders, and he pushed your left shoulder back. The pulling back motion of the left shoulder will turn your right shoulder under your chin, the same as the handshake would, but now the attention is fully in your left shoulder.

I do this for several reasons. First, most left-handed golfers are naturally left-handed. They will have more feeling and coordination in their left side because that's their natural hand. They may "click" better with this motion than that of the right shoulder starting back. Maybe their turn will feel more natural and be easier to repeat, which of course is very important to a consistent swing. The left hand usually has more strength and can guide the club a little more accurately.

The other reason has to do with swinging the club back on line correctly. Every once in a while, when a student has worked on their handshake for some time, an error starts to occur which could lead to potential problems. What may happen is that during the right hand's pushing of the club back, the clubhead may start going back outside the line. Instead of the club going back down the target line (the line parallel to your feet), then swinging inside slightly, the right hand pushes the club out too much. Instead of the shaft reaching the waist high point in your swing parallel, it's now pointing outside the line. This can result in too upright of a backswing and a lack of shoulder turn. The arms are doing too much and the body isn't doing enough. In addition to the club going back off line, there's not going to be much power, as the shoulders aren't turning like they should. By pulling the left shoulder behind you, the shoulders immediately start turning, and the club goes back slightly to the inside as it should. You must be careful that the left shoulder doesn't pull the club back too far inside but this rarely happens.

What you'll feel is a deeper turn, with your upper body really coiling around your legs. The left shoulder pull isn't any more correct than the right shoulder push. It's just an option that may work better for you. Try them both and see what's best.

Tying the Handshake and Wall Together

The handshake and wall make your job pretty easy by giving you two simple words to think of. There are many different parts of the wall and handshake, but these two words sure do a lot of good things for you. There's the zipper to think about on your downswing but only these two during the backswing motion. Well, if two thoughts are better than three, then one is better than two.

One of my favorite moves or

thoughts is; turn your right shoulder over your left knee. When you're standing over the ball I think a great swing thought is to get your right shoulder to turn enough that it lines up with your left knee. This easy thought gets your shoulders turning as they do during the handshake, or when you pull the left shoulder back behind you. It also does a good job at keeping your wall solid. There's no way your right shoulder will get over your knee if your shoulders don't turn as they should, and there's no way your right shoulder will line up with your left knee if you knock the wall over. If the left knee juts out laterally and your wall collapses, the right shoulder can't catch it. The left knee moving out a few inches would make it impossible for the right shoulder to catch it. Pulling the left shoulder back around the left leg is another thought that you can try. A third way to work on your shoulder turn would be to think, "turn your back to the target." If your torso turns enough so your back is actually facing the target, you've made a great shoulder turn. A tour pro like Phil Mickelson turns so much that his back actually faces into left field. His back not only gets to the target, but turns past it some 20 degrees. This huge turn aids in his great length off the tee with seemingly little effort. A senior player with reduced flexibility may not be able to achieve a turn like this, but trying to turn will increase his chances for a more powerful stroke.

The Advanced Downswing

If you review the chapter on the downswing you'll see that there are many ways to begin your forward motion through the ball. You could think turn your zipper, or turn your hips, or turn your knees, or kick your left knee in toward the ball. You also learned to pull your right shoulder out of the way which is still one of my favorites. Getting up on your left toe, or getting your knees together are two others that also work quite well. Well we're again going to think of our left side as we just did on the last few pages.

When you're at the top of your swing, your new idea can be, "lower your left shoulder down and into the ball."

Drive your left shoulder down toward the golf ball and you'll find that your lower body is moving first, as it should. Lowering the left shoulder is the same as pulling your right shoulder. It's just using your left side. You may like this idea for the reason that it again is using your natural left side. If your left shoulder is going down then your right shoulder is going up and out the way. At impact, your left shoulder will be very near to hitting your chin, and your head is staying behind the ball quite well. I also use the expression, "Hold the phone." This expression applies since your impact position will resemble the motion of cradling a telephone between your left ear and left shoulder. You know what you do when you're talking on the phone and you pick up a pencil and paper to write a message. You wedge the phone between your ear and shoulder and squeeze it with your neck. This cradling position very closely matches the impact position of the tour pros. Their rear shoulder is definitely lower at impact than their lead shoulder is, and the angle of their spine is now near 30 degrees, as in

Photo 76: Spine angle is near 30 degrees .

Photo 76.

Getting your shoulders more up and down, or vertical at impact, is an important matter for you to understand, and mastering this new feeling can only lead to advancing your golf swing.

At address your shoulders are nearly level or horizontal to the ground with the left shoulder tilted down some 10 degrees. The tilt, as we discussed in depth earlier, is one of the more important elements in your golf swing. Never, ever forget it. The tilt is created because the left hand is lower than the right when you grip the golf club. During the backswing, the shoulders will turn on this same level, with one shoulder staying at the same height relative to the other. For argument's sake, let's just say the shoulders turn back nearly level. At impact however, this tilt has significantly increased to nearly 30 degrees, with your left shoulder being much lower than the right. Your shoulders are more vertical than they are horizontal at this point and your telephone is wedged securely between your left ear and

Photo 77: This drill keeps the head back longer, lowers the left shoulder down and through the ball with power.

shoulder. Most amateurs mistakenly think that the shoulders are supposed to turn back level, and turn through level. This simply isn't the case. Just looking at any picture of a Tour pro in the impact position will show you that his back shoulder is much lower than his front. I like to think, "Turn level, turn vertical."

Getting the left shoulder to lower into the ball also allows you to stay behind the ball better, and keeps your head back a bit longer. It keeps your wrists cocked longer into the downswing, which retains the angle between your arms and club better. With this angle retention, the club will explode into the ball at the last possible second and rifle the ball down the fairway. You don't really need to think about it, it just happens. Picture a coat hanger hanging on the rack. The hook part is your head and the two outside edges are your shoulders. If you push down slightly on the left edge of the hanger the right edge will swing up. If you push the right side up slightly, the left side goes down, with the hook remaining in place. It's the same thing that will happen to your shoulders. Your head stays quite still as the shoulders do their thing. This left shoulder drive also gets you down into the ball better and keeps your body from raising up and hitting the ball thin.

Many times I will hold a club against my student's head (See *Photo 77*) and have them take a swing. The club may bother you mentally, but it won't interfere with your swing. When I do this, the student automatically keeps her head back a bit longer, and lowers her left shoulder down and through the ball with great power. She's still driving her lower body forward toward the target, but is no longer getting her upper body out too far ahead of the ball. If there's any trick to understanding the golf swing better, it may be just that.

The lower body must initiate the downswing and shift the weight toward the right leg, but the upper body must stay back until the ball has been struck. This is crucial to successful ball striking. Let me give you an image to think about.

Picture yourself standing at your address position. Your feet are anchored to the ground and a clamp is holding your head. Your head is nearly over your left knee because of the shoulder tilt. During your backswing your head and lower body will stay still as your torso turns back 90 degrees.

From this position at the top of your swing, the lower body now drives forward, (zipper turn) and turns your hips toward the target. The key though, is your head must stay back where it was at the top of your swing. It's like someone's pulling your middle section forward but your feet and head are resisting and staying back. At impact your body will be in a curved position that in golf jargon is known as the "Reverse C." Look at *Photo 76* again. The "Reverse C" is very obvious. The arms and club head are exploding through the ball, but the head is staying back. There's no way the clubhead can square up through impact if it doesn't pass your head. If your head is also moving forward, toward the target, your upper body will move out ahead of the ball too much and leave the clubface open, causing a slice.

The arms couldn't roll, the left hand couldn't shake hands, and the clubface stays open because they never had a chance to catch up and pass your head. This is commonly referred to as a blocked shot, or getting ahead of the ball. There must be some point in your downswing that your body is stopping enough so the clubhead can pass it and square the clubface up. Keeping your head back will do the job for you. From this "Reverse C" position at impact, the ball takes off straight at the target and your upper body will then move forward with the rest of your body. You don't stay in the Reverse C all the way through your golf swing, just at impact. A common error many amateurs make is keeping this Reverse C all the way thorugh their swing. Not only is this unnatural but it can cause excess strain on your lower back. At the completion of your swing your body should be straight up and down, with your head, torso, and legs lined up in a straight line. In the early 1970's, staying in the "Reverse C" was popular with golf instructors, but its merits quickly faded. Too many golfers were throwing their backs out and it just didn't make sense to keep half your body back and not drive it forward. Remember, the "Reverse C" is only there at impact to allow your clubhead to square up during contact. As soon as the ball leaves the clubface, the entire body can move up and through into a balanced finish. If there is anything more contradictory in the golf swing, it's this. The lower body and your middle section want to drive forward as much and as fast as it can, but your upper body and head must stay back. Strange but true.

The Path of the Clubhead Through Impact

Now it's time to get technical. What I'm going to discuss in this section may well be the least understood aspect in a golf swing and one that far too few people know and realize is happening. I hope that by the time you're finished reading this section you'll understand fully one of golfs little intricacies that has a tremendous impact on your shot making. Bear with me.

The path of your swing is the line the clubhead travels on. It's like your clubhead is driving down a road full of twists and turns and it must follow along correctly. Don't confuse the "path" of your swing with the "plane" of your swing. The plane is more of the relationship the club has to your body turn and where your arms are. If your arms are higher on your backswing your plane will be more "upright." If your arms are lower and closer to your body your plane is "flatter."

The "path" is what line or road the clubhead is following. What we're going to discuss is the path your club takes during the downswing.

At address, your arms are hanging down limp and natural. They're extended but are not stiff or rigid. The club lays in your hands as you set the clubhead behind the ball. Your arms are no different than they would be if you were just standing still talking to someone.

At impact however, the arms are being stretched out some due to the club swinging down with great speed. The momentum and centrifugal force are making your arms reach out because they're holding onto a club that's traveling 90 or 100 mph in some cases. Because of this, the head of the golf club returns to the ball in a different position than it was at address. With video analysis and high-speed pictures, we can see that the position of the clubhead has been "pushed out" nearly an inch or so as it approaches the ball. In other words, if the clubhead was originally positioned directly behind the ball at address, it has now returned to a position that lines the ball up off the hosel or neck of the golf club, or quite near the shaft. Instead of the ball being in the center of the clubface, it's now toward the shaft of the golf club too much. This of course would result in a shank.

The clubhead is trying to go out to the left a few inches because of the great speed and centrifugal force that is being created in the golf swing. Because your arms are soft and pliable, they stretch out farther than they

Photo 78: Clubface at address.

Photo 79: Clubface at impact with no compensation or correction.

were when they were just hanging there at your address position. Your arms aren't made of steel. They give a little during the swing. The clubhead actually returns to the ball in a position that is outwards of where it started. If you made no corrections or compensations during your swing, you would shank the ball every time. I hope you understand this phenomenon. *Photos 78 and 79* show you what I've just described

Now, even though you may not realize that this stretching is going to happen, your sub-conscious will.

Somewhere in your swing your sub-conscious is going to say, "Hey, if we swing out like this we're going to hit the ball off the neck of the club and shank it." To stop the shank from happening, the brain is going to tell your arms to pull in some on the downswing to try and find the sweet spot. This pulling action with your arms will result in a shot that is pulled off to the right. The only way to stop the clubhead from jutting out to the left was to pull it around to the right. I'd say that more than half the pulls that happen to the average golfer are a result of this action. There are a thousand other reasons a pull may happen as we have discussed, but this one is most common and is the least noticeable.

So, what do we do?

Next time you're on the range, try

Photo 80: Ball positioned off the toe.

hitting shots with your golf ball positioned off the toe of your club instead of the ball sitting directly in the center of your clubface, as in *Photo 80*.

From this position your arms and club can now swing freely through the ball and your club can take its natural path out toward left field a little. Your sub-conscious no longer has to tell you to pull your arms in and around you to find the sweet spot. They can naturally swing fully through the ball and extend out as they should. If your ball is teed an inch toward the toe, the clubhead now has to swing out an inch to find the sweet spot. Your arms can extend fully through the impact position without fear of shanking the ball. Actually, they have to. I call this feeling the "long left arm." If someone took a picture of you half way through your follow through, you'd see that your left arm if fully extended and looks like it's growing. This position is quite noticeable with the Tour pros. Their head is staying back, but their arms look like they're a hundred feet long.

Ben Hogan used to say, "Throw your arms away from you." I like to give the analogy of a baseball batter hitting the outside part of the plate. If he gets his arms extended out over the plate he's going to hit a home run. If the pitcher threw the ball inside to this batter, he'd have to pull his arms in and would never get the extension. The pitcher "jammed" him so he couldn't get the full release of his arms and hit the ball out of the park. Without swinging any harder you'll hit the ball at least ten yards farther now because of this extension. "Long arms" through the swing translates to a long shot.

The golfer who tees the ball in the sweet spot and has to pull his arms in to stop the shank, usually ends up in the "chicken wing" position through impact. The right arm is all bent and crooked and there's no feeling of power. The shot is either pulled to the right, or is pull-sliced off into left field. (See *Photo 81*.)

What it's going to feel like is that you're intentionally trying to push the ball to the left a little. Instead of trying to hit the ball straight, you're going to

Photo 81:The "Chicken Wing."

start the ball into left field a few yards. It's only natural for the ball to take off to the left because that's where your arms are going. The ball will start slightly left of the target, then draw its way back to the target. This is the proper flight of a golf ball for left-handed golfers, left to right.

We've discussed drawing the ball in this book, and we know that we're supposed to, but now realize that the ball should start slightly left. After all, if it's going to curve right some, it's got to start left some. I'd say that most Tour professionals push the ball 5 yards, then draw it back 5 yards. There's certainly nothing wrong with a dead straight shot, but it's technically incorrect. The golf club swings like a circle as it goes around you, so the

143

flight of the ball is just an extension of this circle. I like to think that if you hit a ball while standing on the moon, it would take off and fly 10 miles in a circle then land back on the tee. I know when you've watched golf on TV that the right-handed players look like they shank the ball off the right side of the screen. This is an optical illusion that the camera creates, but the ball does indeed start off to the right before it draws back.

When you first try this on the range I would take a 7 iron and tee the ball. Position the ball entirely off the toe of the club, and hit little half shots trying to push the ball a few yards to the left. It's easier to get the feel of it if you first start with half shots. You may hit the ball too far off to the left at first but that's OK. With a little experimentation you'll quickly get skilled at hitting with about a five-yard push consistently. The reason you'll leave it out to the left is that with the little half shot the ball doesn't stay in the air long enough for your draw to happen. You can work on that later. After you've gotten good at the little shot, try hitting the ball a bit farther each time you practice. Eventually your shots will start toward left center field on a consistent basis, then draw in right onto the flagstick. If you ever shank one it's simply that you exaggerated the pushing motion and overdid it a little. First you have to make it push, then simply allow it to push. You will notice almost from day one that your pull has completely vanished. There's no way the ball will pull to the right if your arms and club push out to the left.

After some time, you can start bringing the clubhead a little closer to the ball because this exaggerated push feeling is becoming more natural. I like to tee the outside edge of the ball even with the outside edge of the clubhead. This position will let your arms swing out as they should without having to jut it out there too much. I think you could play like this for the rest of your life. It's not a quick cure or a gimmick. It's the way to play. Remember: the clubhead always goes out during the downswing, so it must be in some at address.

Some of you may be thinking that the Tour pros don't do this and you're right. Because Tour pros are highly skilled in their ball striking, they can tee the ball directly in the center of the clubface and still not shank it. This is because they get their legs and hips out of the way better and faster than most of us do on the downswing, and create extra room for the club to have room to swing out toward the ball. Because their legs "get out of the way" faster than the average player, the club drops in closer to their body as they start their downswings and can move out through the impact position. Golfers call this, "dropping the club in the slot," and is a move that only the lowest of handicappers can ever master. For the millionth time, just because a Tour pro does something, that doesn't mean you should.

I'd even position the ball toward the toe some on your chips and pitches. In case your head moves forward or your arms push out slightly on the downswing, you'll be protected from shanking the ball off the hosel.

The explanation could get even more technical knowing that shafts bend and flex during the downswing, and that your center of gravity changes as you swing down, but these are issues that just happen and that you have no control over, so why worry about them.

Teeing the ball toward the toe of your club will lead to longer, crisper shots that draw from left to right, and all but eliminate the shank and pull from ever happening.

Incorporate it into your game and you'll notice a difference that is substantial and immediate.

Practice Time

Ben Hogan said two things I've always remembered. First, "There isn't enough time in the day to practice all the shots you need," and second, "Every day you miss playing or practicing takes you one day longer to get good." How true his words were for this game of ours. The pros spend countless hours working on their games to reach the level of near perfection they demonstrate to us on a weekly basis.

But let's be realistic, most of us don't have the time or freedom to play and practice all day. Things like jobs and family are responsibilities we all have and getting to the range a few days a week is the most any of us can expect. With this limited time to work on our games, how and what you should practice is as important as how much you should practice.

For starters, a marathon session on the range of three or four hours is a waste of time. By the end of your session your body will be too tired to perform as it should, and you'll probably start day dreaming too much. It's just impossible to concentrate for that long a period of time. I remember in college some of my professors telling me that the average person has an attention span of under an hour, and anything that drags on too long is difficult to process and understand. That's why day-long lectures have several breaks thoughout the session to give the students a chance to clear their heads and get the blood flowing again. By the second or third hour of hitting balls you'll find yourself experimenting too much and trying things that are unnecessary. You start "messing around" with your swing so much that it's hard to even get back the swing you had when you got there. You try this, and try that, and before long nothing works well. In golf it seems that everything works once. You could stand on your head with your eyes closed and hit one good shot but that probably isn't the swing you want to stick with.

In my own teaching, I spread out the lessons about a week apart. If I teach someone the "handshake" one Saturday, I don't get into the "wall" until the next Saturday. The student needs that week to work on her first lesson and make it a bit more of a natural feeling. It's very difficult for her to learn the "wall" if she hasn't had some time to work on the "handshake." Also, the longer I work with a student I start getting into more and more advanced topics. I start with the basics (the three fundamentals) and then after a year or so, start getting into more advanced moves. Advanced doesn't mean they're harder to execute, it means you first have to learn certain parts of the swing before getting into others. It's like a child going through grade school. They spend a year in first grade before moving on the second. Kids don't learn algebra the day after they learn addition, it takes a while.

If you only had an hour to work on your game, I'd spend about half the time hitting full shots and the other half working on your short game. After you've learned to have a solid, consistent full swing it's really like riding a bike. You're trying to do the same thing over and over again, the same way. Your short game however takes a lifetime of practice to develop your feel and touch. Your touch can leave you at a moment's notice and must be constantly worked on to stay refined. I see this often from many of my Northern students who come to Florida for the Winter. Their full swing is pretty much the same as it was at the end of last season, but they have absolutely no feel for their short game. It is only through endless repetition that your short game can reach the level it should. Technique is pretty easy to duplicate after a long lay-off. It's the touch that needs to be keyed on from day to day. An example would be in chipping. You may still chip your ball straight, solid and crisp, but you hit it way too far past the hole. You didn't do anything wrong in your stroke, you simply hit it too hard. Your next attempt will probably be too short. After a while, your brain starts figuring out what to do and re-learns the feel that you had before you had the lay off.

Green Games.

There are many games you can play on the practice putting green that can help you develop your touch, and make learning and practicing more enjoyable. Let's start with a putting game.

Most practice greens have five or six practice holes on them. Take one ball and work your way around the green trying to two-putt every hole. If you played six holes, you should try for making your way around in 12 strokes or less. A one-putt would be nice from time to time, but try to eliminate any three putts. If you score over 12, go back and do it all again until you can score a 10 or 11. This game lets you not only work on your stroke, but on your ability to read greens and your speed control.

Another game would be to putt to these same six holes trying to never leave any of your putts short or low. I'll bet the first time you go around the green that more than half of your first putts will be short and low, and as we discussed earlier, these putts will never go in. If you make a strong effort to always be on the high side, and a little long, you'll be surprised how many of your putts find the bottom of the hole. They look like they may miss on the high side, but drop it right at the last moment. If you ever leave a putt short or low, make yourself go back and start over again. After one too many times of having to start over, I'm sure you'll get better at leaving your putts long and high, and may even drop in a few along the way.

You could spend some time putting to a dime that you lay on the green. Putting to a dime for 15 minutes will refine your touch even more. Because you're putting to such a small object, it will make the hole look enormous when you actually play. You're so used to hitting the tiny dime that when you look at an actual hole your brain will feel like your aiming for a hula-hoop. You'll feel like you can't miss.

To work on your touch another

way, take 10 balls onto the green. Putt the first ball all the way across the green, let's say 80 feet. Then putt the next ball and leave it 3 feet short of the first ball. Putt the next one 3 feet short of this one and continue this until you've putted all 10 balls. You should have a "string" of balls on the green in a straight line all 3 feet apart. To reverse the game, hit the first ball short, and try to get the other 9 balls 3 feet longer each time. This is also a great game for your pitching.

Pitch one ball about 15 yards and remember what it felt like. Pitch the next ball 20 yards, and the third 25. Do this with ten balls until you can have equal five-yard increments, then do it in reverse hitting the first ball the longest and the others short by five-yard increments each time. This is really the only way you're going to develop any long lasting touch. You're working on your swing and technique some, but are really concentrating on your touch. This way when you're faced with having to hit a 35 yard pitch on the golf course you have some experience to fall back on, since you've hit this shot countless times during your practice sessions.

Bunker Games.

For your bunker play, try to hit 10 shots out to within 10 feet of the hole, and stay there until you do. If your first nine end up inside 10 feet, and your last attempt doesn't, make yourself go back and hit all 10 again. It's kind of your punishment for the last bad one, and quickly teaches your body to respond to the pressure. You're not playing for the Masters or anything, but you don't want to have to keep going back again and again

each time and start all over. Soon, your last shot will start being your best instead of your worst as you learn to respond favorably to the pressure of having to perform.

Full Swing Games.

For your full swing you can also play lots of little practice games. Make yourself hit ten 7 irons to within five yards of the flag. If you miss that last one, go back and hit them all again. Hit ten 3 woods and make them all land in an imaginary fairway that you've outlined on the range. Your fairway could be between two trees on the back of the range some 30 yards apart and all your shots must come to rest within them. You could also play nine holes while staying on the range.

Even though you're on the range, picture your first hole and select the club that you would normally use, let's say a driver. If your first hole goes out and dog-legs from left to right, picture that fairway on the range and try to hit it. If you land in your designated spot, pick the club you'd hit for your next shot and go for your imaginary green. If you miss your fairway, hit your next range ball from a spot on the range that has some rough, since that's where your ball would have ended up on the real hole. Don't fluff up your lie since you're not allowed to do so on the golf course. If your iron shot from the rough hits within your imaginary green, give yourself two putts and go on to the next hole. If your shot lands off your imaginary green, go to a spot and chip a ball the appropriate distance. You're simply playing the whole golf course from the range and are giving yourself a chance to use every club in your bag. You never hit the same club twice in a row when you're on the golf course (unless you hit one out of bounds), so why should you hit the same club twice in a row on the range? You may hit fifty 7 irons in a row when you're working on your swing, but this game is working on your mental approach. The other reason to play the whole course on the range is when you play the actual course you'll be more familiar with it and won't feel so strange actually being out there. There will be no reason to be uncomfortable on the course since you've been there before on the range.

There are dozens and dozens of practice games you can work on to refine your golf game, and lots more that you can invent yourself. Just don't make the mistake of mindlessly hitting balls for no reason. You don't hit ball after ball on the golf course without first analyzing your situation and picturing your shot, so don't do it on the range. There's a big difference between hitting balls and practicing. The pros practice what they'll face on the golf course in a real situation, and think about what they're doing with each range ball. The amateur tends to just hit, and hit and hit, without any thought to what they're doing, and that's a waste of time.

Golf Balls

What kind of ball should you play? Does it really matter? Will you hit that new ball 20 yards farther? The answer is yes and no. Deciding on what type of ball to hit is largely going to be based on how hard you swing and what level golfer you are. A tour professional with an amazing amount of talent and clubhead speed will need a ball that matches up with their game a lot more than the average player will. The pro is good enough to tell the difference, where most amateurs are not. This may be a brutally honest comment but it happens to be true.

Before getting into what ball may be best for your game, let's discuss the golf ball itself. There are of course a million different golf balls on the market, but there are really only two different kinds of balls. These two different balls are called "two piece" or "three piece," or "solid" or "wound."

Most balls made today are of the "two piece," or solid variety, and make up 90% of the market. They're called "two piece" since that's how many pieces comprise the ball itself. The inside, or core of the ball, is one piece, and the cover is the second piece, simple enough. These balls are solid on the inside like an apple is solid when you slice it in two. These balls feel at bit harder when you hit them, and tend to spin less when they leave the clubface. With less spin, they're easier to hit straight, and they roll a bit further when hitting the ground. They go straighter since there's less side-spin, and roll further since there's less backspin trying to stop the ball when it hits the ground. For these reasons amateurs tend to like a ball like this since they're going to hit more fairways and get a bit more roll. Since their covers are also a bit harder they last longer too. You'll lose a ball like this long before you'd ever cut it. For value, duration and distance, this is the kind of ball most folks should be playing.

A good golfer doesn't like a ball like this for exactly the same reasons. A pro wants a ball that he can curve at will, and also wants his ball to stop on the green. A pro doesn't have a wicked slice, and instead wants a ball that will slice if he wants it too. The pro can hit his wedge shot right at the pin, and wants the ball to stop there, instead of rolling over the green. The pro also wants a softer feeling ball to match up with his refined touch around the greens. For all these reasons, the pro plays the "three piece'," or "wound ball."

This ball has a small inner core, about the size of a marble, and is usually made of some sort of soft rubber. Then yards and yards of rubber bands are wrapped around it. This is all covered, making up the three pieces. The rubber bands are tightly wound around the core, and makes the ball not only feel softer, but spin much more. The cover is made from a softer material as well and tends to grab the green better when the ball lands. The traditional cover material for the three-piece ball is called "balata" and is far and away the choice on the PGA tour. The downside to balata is it's so soft that the ball will cut quite easily, and the life span of one of these balls is usually only 18 holes. Most Tour pros use a new ball about every three holes. The ball gets all marked up and can even go out of round, so most average players shy away from them. They also cost at least double the price of the solid balls, so they're not too good of a value. This soft wound ball has a better feeling around the greens and matches up with the superb feel of a Tour professional.

In the last few years, golf ball manufacturers have developed a variety of new balls that combine some of the qualities from both the balls, sort of hybrids, and have given us all more than enough choices to pick from.

There are far too many different balls for this book to discuss in detail. Just know that no company makes a bad ball, and any name brand ball you choose will be just fine. Buy a sleeve of a few different brands and try them out yourself. You'll quickly see that one just feels better to you than the other. Also realize that there is no magic ball that will go 50 yards further. They simply don't exist, or if they do, they're not legal to use in competition. Balls may feel differently, or fly at different trajectories, but they're basically all going to go the same distance in the air. Some may roll farther since they're spinning less, and some may stop quicker since they're spinning more, but most of them go the same distance in the air. They have to. The USGA has very strict guidelines when it comes to their testing of balls and equipment, and anything that goes beyond their range of acceptable is not approved to play with. As your golf game gets better, and your touch and feel become more refined, changing balls may give you the feel you're looking for. Going to a harder ball may give you more distance off the tee, or using a soft ball may get your pitch shots to bite a bit more, but these differences are subtle at the most. Check out the selection of balls in your pro shop and read what the box says. It will give you a brief description of what that ball does, and will key on either more distance or more control, or both. Then talk to the pro about the durability factor, and lastly, look at the price.

Chapter Fourteen:
100 Quotes, Phrases, Analogies, Wisdom

This final chapter is a collection of sayings I find myself using on a daily basis. Many of them I've picked up listening to other professionals or TV announcers. Some are sayings I've invented myself or that I've read over the years. I present them in no particular order, and offer them as tidbits of information that may help you remember a particular swing thought or idea. I could probably come up with thousands of little catch phrases that I've heard over the years, but these hundred are ones that have really stuck with me. I hope you enjoy them.

1. You're not picking your head up, you're standing up.
2. Slower is better than faster.
3. Never up, never in.
4. Your body swings your arms, not the other way around.
5. "If you stand there wrong, you're going to hit it wrong." - Ken Venturi
6. "Throw your arms away from you on the downswing." - Ben Hogan
7. Never think of your arms during the swing.

8. Never look away when you miss a putt. You're being given a lesson.
9. Practice the way you play.
10. Swing like your practice swing.
11. Swing the club, don't hit the ball.
12. The ball gets in your way.
13. Keep it low when you're chipping.
14. You have one swing and 14 clubs, not the other way around.
15. Your legs are the foundation of your swing.
16. Start your lower body down first.
17. Pause at the top.
18. The slowest part of your swing is the change of direction.
19. Swing your driver slower than your pitching wedge. Longer clubs take longer to swing.
20. Your backswing controls your downswing.
21. Finish up on your back toe.
22. Point your belt buckle at the target.
23. Two thirds of golf shots are less than 100 yards from the green.
24. Nearly half your score are putts.
25. Ninety percent of all golfers' clubs don't fit them.
26. Drive for show. When you get out

of the trees, putt for the scorecard.

27. Take it one shot at a time.

28. Don't think about your last shot. There's nothing you can do about it.

29. Beware of a golfer whose back toe is dirty. He's a good golfer.

30. "Keep your flex." - Ken Venturi

31. 90% of golf is mental. - Jack Nicklaus

32. "Keep it low." - Lee Trevino's advice to his amateur partner on putting.

33. When you're chipping, think of bowling. Throw the ball just over the line and get it rolling.

34. Trees are 90% air.

35. If you hook your wood, you're good.

36. "I can talk to a fade but a hook won't listen." -Lee Trevino

37. A push is better than a pull.

38. There's nothing good about a shank.

39. Hit the tee and don't worry about the ball.

40. I'd rather make every ten-foot putt, than hit every drive 300 yards.

41. See the shot in your mind before attempting your stroke.

42. The best shot in golf is always a lay-up.

43. "Don't move your head until you hear your putt drop." -Gary Player

44. "Play three-quarter golf. Swing three quarters of your maximum speed and length." - Ken Venturi

45. Let the wind be your friend.

46. Putt to a spot 10 inches past the hole and let the hole get in the way.

47. "I chip it if I want to make it, and putt it if I want to get it close." -Jack Nicklaus

48. A good grip is crucial to good golf.

49. Just lay your hands on the club.

50. Just shoot for the middle of the green.

51. "Ninety per cent of putts left short don't go in." - Lee Trevino

52. A pitch shot feels like an under handed throw.

53. Remember, shiny like glass is with the grain.

54. Grain grows away from the mountains, and toward the water.

55. Your back heel must be off the ground before impact.

56. Unless your left arm is longer than your right, your left shoulder must be lower than your right.

57. When you get in trouble, get out in one shot. That's your main job.

58. Look where you want to hit the ball, not where you don't want to hit the ball.

59. There's no break on a three-foot putt.

60. "My favorite club is the rake." - Don Anderson

61. The guy who wins the tournament is putting and chipping the best.

62. Three-putting generally ruins most holes.

63. Fairways and greens, fairways and greens.

64. The golf swing is like a roller coaster. It goes up slow, pauses at the top, then comes down real fast.

65. Losing your balance is your body's way of telling you you're swinging too fast.

66. Keep your chin up at address so your shoulders have room to turn.

67. Wiggle your toes when you're waggling your club.

68. Leaning on your toes will make you pull the ball.

69. Golf is a two-handed game.

70. Irons off the tee for safety.

71. Your legs just stand there and you turn your shoulders around them on

the backswing.

72. Turn your back to the target, then turn your chest to the target.

73. Close the gap between your knees to liven up your legs.

74. Your zipper will point where the ball goes.

75. Start with slow motion swings before swinging all out.

76. Stand on two 2 x 4's when you swing and try to keep your balance.

77. You don't need to be big and strong to hit the ball far. You need to be flexible.

78. Turn your right shoulder under your chin on the backswing.

79. You'll never always use the same swing thought. They change over time.

80. Watch out for a golfer that's been sick. His tempo will be better and he'll play great.

81. Hit balls with your feet close together, you'll feel the motion of your arms.

82. Make the clubhead pass your head on the downswing.

83. "Swing around a steady head." - Jack Nicklaus

84. The head is the center of your swing, like the axle is the center of your tire.

85. Take an extra club and swing easier.

86. Get to the range at least a half hour before you tee off. Warming up is crucial.

87. Don't give yourself putts. When you're in a tournament, you'll have experience putting the little ones.

88. Don't watch your partners' swing…they may rub off on you.

89. Know the rules. Ninety-nine per cent of the time they only help you.

90. Tee off first and put the pressure on your opponent.

91. "If you practice Monday through Saturday and take off on Sunday, you've lost the whole week." - Ben Hogan

92. Have a golf club in your hands every day, even if it's swinging or putting indoors.

93. All putts are speed putts.

94. If you have any doubt that you'll make your putt, you won't make it.

95. It doesn't matter what brand of clubs you play, it matters if they're sized correctly for you.

96. It's easy to hit the ball long, and easy to hit the ball straight. But it's hard to hit the ball long and straight.

97. People tend to practice the most with the club they hit the best.

98. Practice from every conceivable lie when you're on the range. You never know what you'll get on the course.

99. "The longest walk in the world is from the practice tee to the first tee."- Ken Venturi

100. Remember. It's just a game.

And Finally …

My profound wish is that this book helps you in understanding the complex action of swinging a golf club. There is no greater joy for the teacher than to see his students improve and start enjoying themselves in the greatest game of all. The lessons on your full swing and short game have been presented in a way that I hope clicks with everyone, and you can cut strokes off your score quickly and consistently. Working on your short game and understanding what to look for in your next set of clubs will no doubt make you a better student of the game. I hope you become something of an expert in analyzing your own game. I think the number one goal of any teacher is to teach you to be able to teach yourself. I hope, if your swing starts going bad in the middle of your round, you now will have the ability to fix it yourself and finish strong.

As I was writing this book, I was constantly struck at the vast amount of knowledge one needs to develop a sound golf swing, and how long it takes to learn everything there is to know about this game. Even Jack Nicklaus says he still learns something new every time he plays 18 holes.

Practice without purpose, or without a plan is, and will always be, a waste of time. Spending some time working on specific goals however, can be a truly rewarding experience as you see yourself progress and start hitting the ball better than you ever have before. Learning the game of golf can be one of the most frustrating endeavors you'll ever attempt in your life, but sticking with it and applying your knowledge can lead to that one perfect round you've dreamed about and can become one of life's greatest joys. I've hit home runs, bowled strikes and have run for touchdowns before, but nothing rivals the feeling of hitting a golf shot perfectly and watching it soar down the fairway. I can still remember the first time I actually broke par, and the feeling of utter contentment and pride that I had inside. It's like I had accomplished something very rare in life and couldn't wait to go out and see if I could do it again. Golf can be addictive, and I can think of no better way to spend your leisure time than enjoying a fine, eighteen holes of golf on a sunny day.

You can take the knowledge you have learned from this book and continue working on it over the years, and share it with your own pro during a lesson with him. Tell the pro what you're trying to accomplish, and the feelings you have. He can help you achieve it, or can enhance what you're already working on. PGA professionals are dedicated to improving your golf games, and are always glad to hear new pieces of information that may enhance their teaching skills.

Here's wishing you continued success in the future and remember this, dear lefties:

YOU'RE STANDING ON THE RIGHT SIDE OF THE BALL!

Acknowledgements

This book would not have been possible without the help of a long list of friends, old and new. But I would especially like to thank Rich Lamb for letting me do my own thing, and giving me the chance to know you. You're the best.

Thanks to Tom Wallace, Head Professional, and the entire Eastwood Staff; the PGA of America, especially Jamie Roggero and Chris Hunkler; Jim Butler and the staff at the Forest C.C.; the gang at "Lumpys," the best golf shop in the world; to Mark Johnson at Left-TeeGolf.com; to John Dill, thanks for the great title; to Lori Salem for the great photos; to Bill Underwood for the opportunity; to all my friends and students; and finally to Paul deVere for your knowledge, guidance, insights and world-class writing skills. I literally could not have done it without you.

"The Lefties"

Left to Right: *Edna Mudry, age 65, handicap 8; Ward Kagan, age 16, handicap 10, Andrea Ballantine, age17, handicap17; The Author, age 41, low round. 62.*

To contact Steve Anderson for information or lessons, visit *www.steveandersongolf.com.*